I Live On an Island

Other books by Catherine de Hueck Doherty
published by Ave Maria Press:

POUSTINIA

THE GOSPEL WITHOUT COMPROMISE

NOT WITHOUT PARABLES

SOBORNOST

STRANNIK

I Live On an Island

Catherine de Hueck
Doherty

Ave Maria Press · Notre Dame, Indiana 46556

Library of Congress Catalog Card Number: 78-74433
International Standard Book Number: 0-87793-170-4 (Cloth)
0-87793-171-2 (Paper)

© 1979 by Ave Maria Press, Notre Dame, Indiana 46556

Cover photo: Thomas Cajacob
Art: Joyce Stanley

Printed and bound in the United States of America.

Contents

Introduction

I live on an island.

Since I live alone, I can understand how it is that my weakness is God's strength. In a manner of speaking, my weakness, my solitude, is a way of not presenting any obstacles to his using me as an instrument of his designs and his grace. It is something I would not have been able to learn as easily elsewhere. But there are more lessons of the Lord here, as I presently hope to explain and share with you.

I can see the mainland quite easily. When the sun is at its brightest, the white buildings of Madonna House glisten like gems set securely in the green of the fields and the blue of the Madawaska River.

At night, this gem-like radiance shines out from within, flooding through the many windows, creating the impression (which is not too erroneous) that Madonna House is really a little village of its own.

I can also see the main building, with our libraries, chapel, kitchen, dining room. Over there is St. Clare's and St. Veronica's: small wooden cabins that are reserved for the sick and for members of our family who are tired and need a little rest for a weekend or so. St. Veronica's, at one time, served as a gift shop; we called it the P. X. There we sold many of the beautiful things that came to us as donations from our good friends; we also sold some of our own handicrafts. The money was used to pay for the ambulances that took the poor sick to the hospital.

I can see the rather large building that almost dwarfs Madonna House itself. We have named it St. Goupil's in honor of the layman who accompanied the Jesuit martyrs. We have a great devotion to him. Upstairs in St. Goupil's is a women's dormitory; downstairs the laundry, sewing room, one of our offices. In the basement is one of the men's workshops.

A little farther away is St. Peter's, another wooden cabin originally built for priests. (Eventually they outgrew it.) It now houses several of our laymen. Not far from this is Blessed Martin's cottage, which comprises our dispensary and our sick bay. Still a little farther, on a small hill, is St. Martha's where another office is located. Here *Restoration,* our monthly newspaper, has its home. Upstairs, more of our women live in a small dorm. The basement of St. Martha's used to be a room to which half the countryside came for much-needed clothing. Now they come to St. Joseph's House, our local mission down the road.

From my island I can see even farther than that. I can pick out Carmel Hill a mile or more away—a farm that now belongs to us. It is home for several men of Madonna House. In the evenings a cozy light twinkles from their old farmhouse. On that hill also is now located our Priest Guest House (Vianney House we call it). Some of our own priests live here, and hundreds of priest guests stay with them each year. I bless this house each night as I cross my bridge to the island.

Not with my bodily eyes, but with the eyes of my soul and mind, I can see even farther—five miles south. There we have a working farm which we named "St. Benedict Acres" after that famous monk and his sons.

Three miles southwest is St. Anne's, where the male guests and volunteers reside. It is also a converted farmhouse. It was named St. Anne's because originally it was a dorm for women. But I don't think the men mind having our Lord's grandmother watch over them!

Thus it happens that each time I look out my window I can behold the works of the Lord, for it would be foolish of me—even for one instant—to think that I had done much to create this now rather vast apostolate. My island teaches me that we are all simply instruments in God's hands. I am not a very good instrument; I am a rather poor one, offering him only my flaming desire to be an obedient, pliant instrument of his love and his will.

This truth—this simple, awesome truth—entered into me very forcibly on the night of December 8, 1960. The *Pro Ecclesiae et Pontifice* medal had just been presented to me in our parish church (which I can also see clearly from my little island). That night, when I returned from the bustle of the ceremony and reception back to the silence, my island seemed to whisper to me: "Now you know for sure that your tremendous weakness is God's strength, and that he has used you, in his infinite mercy, to create this humble apostolate of Madonna House, to further the loving ends of his Father through the Holy Spirit and our Blessed Lady of Combermere. Arise, bow low as is the custom of your people in Russia. Thank him for the unfathomable privilege of his choice."

This I did. I suppose I have a very wise island. It teaches me, very simply, the tremendous truths of our faith.

Practical men might deem these thoughts the product of an overwrought imagination. Maybe so. But who will deny that to a loving and listening heart, to a soul in love with God, everything speaks of him? Could I relate to you what I "hear" if I didn't hear anything? Or tell you what I "see" if I didn't see anything? No.

I simply invite you to come to my island in your imagination and sit quietly here by my fireside. The curtains have been drawn back from my large window. Listen with your heart, as I do. We shall be silent, both of us. But I pray that each one of you will return whence you came, refreshed and more at peace, ready to meet the noises and confusion of daily life with a quiet heart.

Spring

This is the time in-between the winter and the spring. The trees show forth some buds but there is no green and few pussy willows. It is as if all nature were waiting. Waiting for what?

At night, from my side window, I see a thousand stars reflected in the dark waters of the river. The stars seem to be dancing in the water. Probably a stray, gentle wind came from somewhere to stir the waters and make the stars dance. Is it the dance of the heralds of a great king? Are they skipping and dancing like the children who cried on Palm Sunday, "Hosanna to the Lord, Hosanna to the meek one who comes on an ass"? Who can tell? But the stars do dance, and I can see them from my island, and they *are* messengers of a great joy.

In the distant hills here and there I can see lights in the windows of the little farmhouses that dot the wooded hills. The night is dark except for the dancing stars in the waters of my river and the light that springs so suddenly in the darkness. It reminds me of the Easter Vigil, the Paschal Candle, the Holy Fire lit by the priest.

Soon! my heart cries. Soon! say the lights in the hills. Soon! say the stars dancing in the river. Soon life will appear, as the Lord came forth from the tomb. Yes, yes, soon!

But the next day comes and the earth of my island is still brown, lifeless. The trees have not budded yet. The sun barely shines. There is a mystery and a greyness about

the island, as if it wanted to tell me that this is the time of
sorrow, the time of conflict between light and darkness. A
time of pain that stems from a passionate love. This is Holy
Time, hushed time, the time of God's passion in which he
writes in characters of blood a love letter to all of us.

It is a time of silence, a time of recollection, a time of
prayer. The trees wait to bud. The brown earth longs to
sprout its fine greenery, and I learn from it tremendous
lessons about God, about love, about time, about eternity.

*   *   *   *   *   *   *   *   *   *

The few warm days we had in March were buried
under a blizzard the likes of which we had seldom seen for
that time of year. My sturdy log cabin shook under the
violence of a northern wind. A combination of hail and
snow played strange music on my windows through the
angry night. I slept uneasily. I finally woke up, made
myself a cup of tea, and listened to the storm unleashing
itself with an ever-growing fury.

What the exact reason was that made me fall on my
knees that night in March before an icon of Our Lady, I do
not know. I am unable to say. But suddenly I thought of the
justice and anger of God. I reflected on the thoughtless-
ness, the complacency, the indifference of so many people
to whom the words of Christ apply: "The tepid and lukewarm I will vomit out of my mouth." Does it seem foolish
that I shook as if I had a fever, and that I felt the judgment
of God?

Does it seem strange that I wanted to cry out as Moses
did? As the prophets did? Strange, isn't it, to implore the
Lord to forgive all of us, all the millions of people who
never give him a thought, yet who belong to him, bear his
name by reason of their baptism? Does it seem strange that

I found my face wet with tears? I had a desire to stay the hand of his justice and to open the hands of his mercy and forgiveness.

That is what happened on that stormy night on my island. How long did I pray? I cannot tell. I know that when I got up from my knees I was weary, but I still could not sleep. I went out for a moment, perhaps just for a breath of fresh air. But the wind caught me up and almost made me stumble, so I went back into the cabin.

My tea was cold. I made some fresh tea and drank it slowly, but it didn't make me warm, though my cabin itself was warm. I felt cold. And for some reason or another my thoughts turned to poverty. It seemed to me I could see the millions of people who had gone to bed on this dark night, so hungry they couldn't sleep. At the same time, I could see the millions gorging themselves unnecessarily in expensive nightclubs, restaurants and cafes.

I remember the time I was a waitress in a swanky hotel. The leftovers from the tables of those who had dined were so plentiful that they could have fed hundreds of people someplace where hunger was rampant. I remembered watching women play with their food, take a bite out of a T-bone steak and leave the rest untouched. I remembered being disturbed then at the tremendous waste of food in our land, for I have often been hungry in New York, Chicago, Toronto and Montreal.

Yes, I thought of poverty, of all the unnecessary things that clutter our homes that could be given away, and the money given to feed the hungry of this world.

The wind rose in intensity. It seemed to me that I heard hell laughing, and Christ weeping. Spring was late this year in coming to my island.

*   *   *   *   *   *   *   *   *   *

Gone is the greyness of winter days. Gone are the sharp contrasts of sun and snow, a sun that doesn't warm but only shines. Soft pastel shades tint the evenings of spring and the early morning, bringing new hope, new life, especially in the hearts of those who live in the midst of nature.

So it is with the Church, the people of God. The bitter winter storms that followed Vatican II seem a thing of the past. The cold shock of priests leaving the Church, nuns going to beauty parlors and adorning their "cells" with chintz curtains and expensive beds is tapering off. Catholic magazines, as if weary of their negative approach, seem to allow the hard snow of their cold criticisms to melt, too. Slowly, everyone is taking a second look and seeing that the luminous light of eternal hope and the eternal spring of the Church is still with us.

Hope is like the sap rising in the trees. Easter reminds us that Christ is truly risen, and that all Christians have life in the risen Christ. Each member of the Church lives in the resurrected Christ, the Lord of time and eternity. Slowly the snow of doubts, confusion and criticism is melting away; the essence of these attitudes now once again becomes more apparent. More and more people are talking about love. More and more people begin to realize that in order to implement and incarnate Vatican II, all of us must begin with ourselves and must preach the gospel with our lives.

Spring has come to the land. The turtledoves are heard. The fig tree is blossoming. This is the time when all Christians should become lovers of God and of one another. If they do, they will change the magisterium as the magisterium needs changing. They will bring fire on earth, influence governments, economics, nations, as great men have done for ages, and as only a handful of Christians did when they died in the arenas.

Unless each one of us begins to love, and to serve both his brother and his enemies, there will be no real change in the world, except a change for the worse. All reforms, all true revolutions, begin with a few people who are passionate about the reform. Let each one of us be one of these few! Then, we shall indeed renew the face of the earth.

Luminous is the light of spring on my island. Luminous is the light of the resurrected Christ. Let us enter into this light of the Lord who brings us the spring of hope, eternally renewed. He brings us the gift of faith that can grow by leaps and bounds. He brings us the love that can change the whole world if only we incarnate it as he wishes us to.

Alleluia, spring has come to the land! Let us allow that spring of faith, hope and love to come to our hearts as well.

*   *   *   *   *   *   *   *   *   *

My thoughts today go back 10 years—to a trip to Montreal. I had the privilege of lecturing to our French Canadian brothers and sisters. Shortly before that, I had spent some time in Chicago, that sprawling city of the Midwest that is pulsating with life. I met a variety of people, talked to various groups, immersed myself ever deeper into the problems of humanity. When I returned here to my little Canadian island I tried to sort out the ideas, the feelings, the impressions that I had accumulated during my travels.

Why did I find this sorting so painful? On the one hand, it lifted me up to great heights from which, a heart filled with gratitude, I thanked God. For I witnessed in those cities a new Pentecost. The Holy Spirit, the Wind that blows so freshly across our earth, was spreading his

fire everywhere in the hearts of men, bidding them to renew
this earth and restore it to God.

On the other hand, while sorting out my impressions,
I plummeted into intolerable dark depths of pain, an
excruciating pain of the spirit that left me bereft of any
words with which to express it. Why did joy, pain, fear,
gladness and sorrow weave this strange tapestry in my
heart?

As I tried to think this out, an answer came: that I had
been living, not in the eye of the hurricane, but in some
strange "center" between the mystery of Iniquity and the
mystery of Light and Love. It had been given to me, by
the grace of God, to realize dimly—but vividly and pain-
fully—that the battle between the mystery of Light and the
mystery of Darkness was going on in the hearts of all men
today in an explosive, intense form, perhaps in a form that
has never, or seldom, been experienced by those who call
themselves followers of Christ.

This battle is so intense in the hearts of Christians
that it spills over, as it were, into the hearts of non-
Christians. As a result of this inner battle between these
two mysteries, the very existence of the world hangs in the
balance.

It came to me also that this is the time when Christians
must pray for one another and for the whole world as they
have never prayed before. At times like this the fine line of
the battle is indeed thin, and souls can tumble onto the
wrong side of this battle line. Yes, it came to me that this is
the time of fasting, prayer and the mortification of all for all.

I myself was torn in the midst of diverse tensions. At
one moment I felt that I should write an article in defense
of the Catholic hierarchy who suddenly seemed to have
become a goad for every avant-garde Catholic to kick
against. Instead of kicking at the bishops we should begin

with hammer and chisel to demolish the walls of that self in us that keeps us from implementing the gospel in our own lives. Yes, I was shuttled like a weaver's shuttle between heights and depths, and it took some time in these moments of quiet on my island to figure out the pattern of the shuttling.

The final result of that trip in me was a hunger, a spiritual hunger, to step aside for a while into solitude and silence, into fasting and prayer. I wanted to cry out from that solitude the cry of the blind man in the Gospel: "Lord, that I may see!"

*   *   *   *   *   *   *   *   *   *

One day a clipping came to my desk which stated:

A survey of 3,000 Roman Catholic priests shows one in four would consider leaving his parish because of severe stress. A study conducted of the Roman Catholic clergy revealed that the priests felt they were under much greater stress than their Protestant colleagues. The survey of the parish priests, conducted by John P. Koval, a sociologist at the University of Notre Dame, showed the generation gap between R. C. clergymen under 45 and those over 50 to be very wide. More than 40% of the young priests polled in the nationwide survey felt so much strain they said they would consider quitting, Koval said. He said overall, in the survey, including both younger and older priests, one in four would consider leaving because of stress.

I kept that clipping for a long time because I wanted to pray over it. Today, anthropologists, sociologists, psychologists, psychiatrists, everybody makes surveys. All

publicize their findings—some of which corroborate, some
of which contradict one another. But when I saw this
particular clipping I wanted to pray to open the doors of
those priests' hearts. I love priests. It is really a funny
thing: I have loved them ever since I was a youngster. I
really and truly believe that, in a manner of speaking, they
are other Christs.

I know that Christ has ascended to the Father; it is an
article of my faith. But I also know that he loved us too
much—us poor recalcitrant human beings—to leave us on
our own. He remained with us in the form of Bread and
Wine, the Blessed Sacrament, to be given to us by his
priests.

A priest to me is Christ wishing to be present in our
midst in and through this man he has called to be his priest.
It doesn't seem to affect me at all if priests are sinful or
holy, or anything in between. I understand that they are
men. But frankly, if I am in need of one of them and know
that he is living a sinful life, I would still crawl to him to
get absolution for my sins, or to receive Viaticum if I were
in danger of death.

There came a day during the Russian revolution when
there were no priests—either Roman or Orthodox—left in
Petrograd. They had all been killed or were in prison.
When there are no priests one realizes their value—and it
doesn't matter if they are in sin or not. I think it was then
I realized what a priest meant to me.

Yes, I love priests with a great love. That is why I
kept this little clipping and prayed over it and thought
about the priests it had polled. As I prayed and reflected,
a great tenderness and a warm gentleness filled my soul.
Call me a fool, but it seemed to me that Christ was bending
gently over all those priests and telling them what they
meant to him and who they were in his eyes.

I wondered if these priests had all given up prayer, or neglected to pray their daily office. Was God in their midst when they had answered those questions on the survey? Did they remember the tensions and sufferings Christ went through during his passion when all his beloved apostles copped out, quit, and did not stand with him under his cross? I wondered if these good priests had ever thought of the hardness of the green wood on which Christ was crucified? It wasn't easy for him. His sufferings were very great, but he didn't quit.

I wondered why these priests wanted to quit. At this point of my prayer there was a knock on the door and a lady walked in. She came to talk to me a little bit about her problem. It was very simple: she had an alcoholic husband and she had five children. She told me that her family counsellor, and even her confessor, urged her to separate from her husband. He was not doing her any good. But she said to me: "I can't leave him. I love him. The children love him, too, even though they know what is going on. You know, Catherine," she went on to say, "a marriage is a sacrament. We knew what we were doing. I certainly did. No, I just cannot quit, tensions or no tensions, pain or no pain, poverty or no poverty. No, I cannot quit. I love him."

We talked a little while longer and then she left. There was a buoyancy in her step now. She kept repeating even as she said good-bye, "Yes, Katie, I love him."

I returned to my desk and looked at the beautiful light that comes over my island at eventide these days when spring is around the corner. Sort of a golden light. I asked myself: Was it possible that the tensions of these priests were too great because they didn't love God enough? For a moment I weakened—if one can call crying weakness. I put my arm over that clipping and I cried. I cried for all those priests who didn't cry, who maybe wanted to but couldn't. I cried with those who did cry because they are also human and weak. I cried for the people of God who will be bereft of priests if any or all of that 40 percent leave.

To be truthful, I cried before God, not only with tears but with my voice. I implored him to help those priests to know him, because obviously they didn't know him or they wouldn't think of leaving. Yes, if they knew him they wouldn't leave. I know of no way to do anything about all of this except to pray.

So, dearly beloved Fathers, whoever or wherever you are, all of you being polled by the pollsters, I simply wanted to tell you that I will pray for you. That is all I can do. But dearly beloved ones, it will be a passionate prayer because you are so needed both by God and men.

*   *   *   *   *   *   *   *   *   *

On this beautiful spring day I think I will tell you a story about how Our Lady got angry!

There was once a beautiful abbey, renowned for its singing. Its choir was celebrated throughout the whole medieval world to such an extent that even the king decided to go there for a Mass. He really wanted to hear some good singing, and also because he hoped it would bring him closer to God.

Well, in the midst of all those marvelous voices there was one little monk who desired to sing with his whole heart, but he was tone-deaf! He couldn't carry a tune, poor little guy. He used to lurk around the corners of the choir. He wasn't very big. He enjoyed himself, even if he didn't quite hear the music as it was sung.

The day of the Mass came. Big doings—red carpets and everything. The little monk was there also, in the corner of the choir, trembling with joy at the beauty of the music. Suddenly, he couldn't control himself. He joined in the singing, and the whole choir went to pot! Everybody hearing those wrong notes just stopped and whispered and made all sorts of comments.

In the meantime, in heaven, while all these wonderful people were singing, Our Lady, who sat on a big carpet in front of God, was playing with the little angels and paying no attention whatsoever to the beautiful music that was wafting up to heaven. In fact, periodically, she used to shake her head and redo her long hair. There was something about this "beautiful music" that she didn't quite like. And she was unhappy about it. God the Father frowned; God the Son would come down and sit on the carpet with her; and God the Holy Spirit would hover over her. The angels would be silent. There would be no singing in heaven when Our Lady frowned, and Our Lady *was* frowning on this abbey and its beautiful singing.

But on this particular day she perked up. She put her hand to her ear and bent down. Her face, which is angelic anyhow, and beautiful, just radiated joy. She was so happy that God the Father smiled, God the Son smiled, and God the Holy Spirit waved his wings around, and all the angels sang.

Meanwhile, down on earth, the abbot was getting more furious by the minute. He yanked that poor little monk out of the choir. The king left. Then the abbot confronted the poor little monk: "Get down into the basement," he said, "on the cold floor, flat on your stomach until I tell you to get up. You will pay for your sins."

So the little monk, very obedient fellow that he was, trotted down to the basement and fell flat on the cold floor. Oh, it was so cold, everything was wet and damp. There was no cement in those days and the water dribbled through the stones. The abbot went back to his room, which was quite comfortable to say the least!

Our Lady was, of course, watching all this. She got up from sitting and playing with the angels and—zip!—she descended as only Our Lady can. She stood in front of the abbot. He had on one of those little medieval caps and he tried to cover himself with it when he saw Our Lady.

You should hear Our Lady when she gets angry! Her anger is not recorded in the gospel because she was meek and mild. But when she saw what the abbot had done to that little monk she really talked like a woman can talk when she gets mad. She said to the abbot: "Up! Get up!" Well, the abbot got up really fast. She led the way down to the basement of the church.

"Down on the floor," she said, "flat on your stomach (the abbot had a big stomach) until I tell you to get up. But before that, apologize to this little fellow. The only thing in heaven we accepted was the singing of this monk. He sang with love, but all the rest of you, because of your pride in singing, were singing for your own glory, for the glory of the abbey, and not for the glory of God. So lie down here on your stomach."

Then Our Lady took the little monk and laid him in the abbot's bed. She even sang him a lullaby, and then she departed.

The abbot remained lying on the cold floor. As Mary came back to heaven, everyone knew, of course, what had happened, as they could see everything from heaven.

Then Jesus, the Forgiving One, came over. Jesus said: "Do you think we should keep him there very long?" Our Lady said: "Well, Moses had to talk to God the Father for 40 days. Why not keep him there 40 days?" Jesus looked at his Father, the Father looked at Jesus. They both looked at Our Lady. Then the Holy Spirit embraced her. She laughed, and everybody in heaven laughed and said, as if with one voice, "Oh, let him get up tomorrow." So they dispatched a little angel to tell him to get up the next day. Our Lady can get angry about some of the strangest things!

*　*　*　*　*　*　*　*　*　*

Many call the earth "God's Book of Love for Man." She reveals his secrets to those who take time to search for them. Did not the Lord Christ use examples from the earth for his parables and his teachings? Though I have but a little strip of earth on my island, all of it is that kind of a book. It brings me closer and closer to God every day. God created my island with the rest of the whole universe and found it very good.

Yet, I think of the millions of people on this continent who do not see the beauty in a tree, the beauty in the tracks of animals on the soft earth, the beauty in the opening of a wildflower in the woods. They do not hear the sounds of the birds, the melody of a brook, the musical whisper of trees discussing the wonders of God, the quiet lapping of waters against the river shore.

They have the sense of smell but they are not using it, or maybe they have lost it amidst the stench of our exhausts and the thousand man-made odors of a city of stone. They do not pause in joy and wonderment to inhale the fragrance of freshly cut hay, of a wood fire burning; they do not breathe in the mystery of virgin earth in some shady corner of the forest.

This divorce between man and nature frightens me. We have lost the image of God so clearly seen in nature because all day long we look at our own image, at the things *we* have made. What are machines? What is technology? Merely images of man that other men have made and which men spend their lives watching, using, and taking care of to make more machines. The more man beholds these images, the farther away he slips from God. He makes himself—and his images—into idols of worship —sterile idols, worshiping them to insanity.

As I think this over, my sadness grows. Not that I advocate the abolishing of all machines. No. That would be regression perhaps. What I desire with a great desire is to restore man's contact with nature, so that man finds again his proper place as a creature of God and a lord of the earth and all it contains.

Yes, the month of May is beautiful on my island. It also brings me to the feet of Our Lady, the Mother of May, whose month it really is. In her hands I lay all my sadness. And I implore her to bring her children back to the book of Nature that God has made for us.

*   *   *   *   *   *   *   *   *   *

Springtime is a lonely time for a solitary.

True, my island is a storehouse of the Lord's treasures. But there are days when it seems that all the treasures are tightly and securely locked up. The skies are dark. The winds are strong. The rain is wild and mournful. Then my island becomes a strange desert. At times it seems like a mountain in the desert, and I am alone on that cold and lonely place, buffeted by strange thoughts, encompassed by new pains. Often these come to me even without the rain, winds, and cloudy skies. They did recently, and I wrote a little poem:

The colors
Are of early
Spring:
Grey,
Purple
Violet.
White
Is the little church
Like
A Paschal
Candle;
It stands
On its
Pedestal
Of purple,
Brown
Earth . . .
Alive
In whiteness
And beauty!

*   *   *   *   *   *   *   *   *   *

My island is crowded with people who cry in the night and can't stop crying out to God even in the daytime. The needs of humanity are on my island. They take my sleep away and they disturb my days. Some cry at noon, and some at eventide. Some wake me up from my troubled sleep at any hour of the night.

The needs of priests, especially on our North American continent, seem to cry out the loudest. They are in pain, in doubt. They are lonely and bewildered. I love them so. I have loved the priesthood ever since I was a child.

Long ago and far away, when I was 12, a fatherly Jesuit gave us a retreat. He told us to pray for priests and someday, when we grew up, to offer ourselves as holocausts for them. Even then I was an impatient character! So I asked him then and there why I had to wait. He tried to tell me, but I kind of brushed his explanation aside with the naivete of childhood.

He asked me if I really wanted to offer my life for priests. Very simply I answered, "Oh, yes, Father. I want to do it now and not wait until I grow up." So he told me to kneel down. I did, and recited some kind of prayer. I have forgotten now what I said, but one thing I knew: from then on my life somehow belonged to priests.

And here they are now, crying out to me on my island, stretching their hands out to me. A fantasy? A hallucination? I wouldn't know. All I know is that their pain is mine, their loneliness is mine. Their doubts are mine, and also their bewilderment. The only thing I don't seem to be able to share is their anger. I take this, however, and lift it in the chalice of my hands for God to change into his peace.

What can I do? Only weep and pray and love and hope and ask the Lord to bring them to Madonna House where they may touch this love of ours for the priesthood; so that perhaps in the mirror of our love (for I am not the only one here who loves them) they may find the peace of the Lord, their role, their identity.

Nuns also cry out on my island. Because they are women, their wounds may be deeper, or seem deeper to them. So many of them leave their religious orders, and many others want to leave. They seek answers and do not find them. When they leave they have no one to help them adjust to a world that has been closed to them for maybe decades.

As I listen I ask myself: Why is it that religious orders within their spacious motherhouses do not provide help for these people? Why don't they provide holy, well-trained priests to answer their spiritual problems? Why don't they enlist the aid of psychologists and psychiatrists to answer or cure their emotional upheavals? Why isn't there a group of nuns set aside to give them understanding love? If this be done, perhaps many would stay and help to change whatever needs changing in their orders. And those who felt in conscience that they still had to leave would be enabled to adjust themselves to that "great outside," that competitive, technological world that will neither understand nor really help them.

Some of these nuns have come to Madonna House. We have priests here to help priests, but no nuns to help nuns. We hope we have helped some, but my island is crowded, Madonna House is crowded. So many thousands of people pass through here, all with problems. We hope we have helped some.

I realize more and more as I travel, as I keep vigil, as I pray, that what the world needs is not more projects, more apostolic works, more works of mercy, more social works, more community development programs. What it needs most today is communities of love, little islands flung everywhere by the hand of God so that men may, like St. Thomas, touch the wounds love always makes.

Today Madonna House is sending out young people by threes and fours to form these little communities of love, to answer without words the million and one questions that arise in the hearts of men—to witness by being. Yes, that is perhaps why my island is so crowded these days: so many people are coming to us to touch the wounds made by Love to be healed of their own wounds.

I must be truthful with myself: I want to escape from

this solitude, from these thoughts, from this pain. But I mustn't, because my facing it will allow me to lift it up to God. This is the only gift that I, who am so poor, can give him, the Crucified.

When the trouble occurred in Selma, Alabama, some years back, I could not go there—I, who had labored in Harlem for so many years. I could not go to Selma—I, who have shared the dreams of my black friends, dreamed with them amid the noise, the poverty, the segregation, the stench of Harlem. So I had to bear the pain of not going, while I also bore the pain of being there. For I was there in everything except my body. In some undefinable way I went with those who went there. I was blinded, nauseated by gas that never reached my face or my lungs. I was drenched by the rain. I was filled with the joy of such sharing. And as I beheld the faces of my white brothers covered with gas masks, I fell on my knees. Yes, in my agony I was able to pray for them. I couldn't go to Selma, but I was there.

At some time—I forget whether it was night or day— I was crucified in my solitude on a strange cross, the cross made by Christians across the world, but especially here in North America. They are the Christians who hate one another, who jeer at one another and laugh and persecute their brothers and sisters because the latter speak of peace in a world poised for war. I cried out to God, to the Lord of Peace, to come down, to send the Holy Spirit into the hearts of those who did not see that war never solved anything. Love does. Love speaks softly, is patient, gentle, understands all things and forgives all things.

I was crucified once again on the free will of men. The Holy Spirit was abroad, but the hearts of men were closed against him. And men refused the peace of Christ. They chose, or seemed to choose, strife and war.

In my solitude and silence I also knew the hunger, the bodily hunger of the world. I was naked with the naked. I was a child dying on the sunny streets in the dry dust of India. I was a Vietnamese youth whose parents were killed in an air raid and who wandered dazed across familiar fields. I was sick in a ghetto in Latin America and no one cared. I knew the loneliness of the old who live alone in little dark rooms in the slums of our modern cities. I *was* all the poor, all the forgotten, all the lonely of the world. I was numb with pain. I had no voice left to cry out. All I could do was open myself wide to the sufferings of all my brothers and sisters everywhere.

Lord, I have nothing to give you but this pain, for I am so poor before you. Accept it, for I give it in the chalice of my love for you and through you to all my brothers and sisters across the world.

*   *   *   *   *   *   *   *   *   *

The birch trees, with great shyness, are beginning to show their leaves, but they are not yet unfolding. They are like tender girls whose promise of great beauty has not yet revealed itself. All around me the color of the mountains is changing, quietly, gently, slowly—changing from purple to green.

For some unaccountable reason, this spring reminds me of springtime in Palestine, the land where the fig tree blossoms in March and the turtledoves are heard in the land. This year's gentle northern spring makes me think of a young girl only 14 years old—Mary, the Mother of God. I rest in that meditation. But suddenly and violently it is disturbed.

It seems as if the sun has vanished from my island. The mountains that only a moment ago gave me joy now

look menacing and foreboding. The water of my river
which was gloriously blue has become bleak and black. I
am no longer far away in Palestine where the fig trees are
blooming and the voice of the turtledove is heard. I'm
back in the year 1967, at the Lay Congress in Rome, at
which Mary was not mentioned. We are, alas, in a time
when Mary is downgraded—almost eliminated—from the
devotions of the post-Vatican II Church.

I would like to analyze the word "devotion," but I
won't. It is not a word I particularly like. Coming from
Russia, I don't consider myself as having a "devotion" to
Mary. I have something far greater, far more immense,
far more beautiful. I have an unshakable faith that she is
the Mother of God and hence the Mother of men. I believe
that she fashioned the body that comes to me as the body of
her son in Holy Communion, and that this body is my bond
with all my fellow Christians and with all humanity.

Mary only said one word—*fiat*—and she said it in
faith, in God. She did ask one or two questions, but then
she immediately accepted the will of God. She accepted it
without understanding, as a few years later she accepted
without understanding the reply of Jesus in the temple.
Mary did the one thing our modern generation refuses to
do—"she kept all his words in her heart." It was in her
heart where the seeds of Jesus' words grew on fertile soil.
And then, one day, she understood.

We are downgrading Mary, downgrading the "woman
clothed with the sun, standing on the moon, with the stars
around her head." We are downgrading the woman who
the Father said would crush the head of the serpent with her
heel. We are downgrading her who is the image and
mother of the Church. Oh, yes, we seek to penetrate the
mysteries of the scriptures, and so we should. But the the-
ologians should also, like Mary, take time to keep all the

words of the Lord in their hearts. Then they will know God as Mary knew him. They will not only know *about* God, but they will know *God himself*.

God is a mystery. No one has seen the face of God and lived, except those who approach him with the heart of a child. These, like Mary, have kept his words in their hearts, and God has come to them and revealed the secret of his words.

* * * * * * * * * *

The river flows around me, silently, waiting for something to happen, listening for someone to come. Silence surrounds me on all sides and makes me meditate.

Strangely enough, this silence brings the roar of traffic to my island. The constant noises of the city surround me. The constant ringing of telephones, the swish of elevators, the unending sound of steps outside office doors, voices that never cease, the muted rumbling of buses, subways and cars.

Whenever I come back to my island from whatever work I do on the mainland, I begin to savor the utter quiet of eventide, and I find myself in the city, the city that never sleeps, where I learned to sleep in spite of all the noises. It is then I begin to pray for all humanity. It seems that very soon now the center of all our lives (with the exception of a few) will be urban centers, cities that extend solidly from one city to another, eating up all the green land in between.

Where then will modern man find the silence, the solitude that he must have, and without which he will not be able to survive the rat race of his urban living? Yes, where? If we are to engage in dialogue with one another, with members of other faiths, with members of our own families and communities, we must learn to listen. For there will be no real dialogue without listening. But in order to be able to listen one must have time for silence and solitude. The listening required is the listening of the heart, a heart that is utterly open to the Holy Spirit. It is in him alone that we can communicate and dialogue with one another.

It was in the silence of my island that I suddenly understood why, quite a few years ago, we of Madonna House transformed an abandoned farmhouse into a hermitage, a desert, or, as the Russians say, a *poustinia*. (The poustinia has since become more widely known through the publication of my book by that name.*) I remember well why this idea came to me. It came because I realized that the members of our apostolate of Madonna House, being deeply inserted into the secular society, had to have a place into which they could retire to be alone in solitude and silence. First, they had to stem the noise within themselves. There is not a modern man or woman living who, in our tense society, is not filled, in one way or another, with that inner noise, a sort of fragmentation of oneself.

When I first proposed this idea of the poustinia everyone was agreeable, but a little astonished, and a bit bewildered. After a few personal experiences in the poustinias, understanding came. To date, we have about 15 of these simple, poor, humble log cabins to which people can go for a day of prayer, fasting and solitude. This inspiration of the Holy Spirit has been confirmed by the extent to which the poustinia experience has caught on among so many thousands of people.

Many people, as a result of reading my book, now spend time occasionally in solitude, on a "poustinia day." We here at Madonna House can only marvel at God's work and praise him that this idea and practice is bearing so

*Ave Maria Press, 1975

much fruit. Yes, spring is coming, the springtime of quiet where all things grow in the silence of God.

*   *   *   *   *   *   *   *   *   *

It came to me one evening—one of those transparent, early spring evenings that only northern countries have— that we all possess within us the key that would prevent us from becoming islands. We all possess the ability, the power, the gift of *prayer*.

Lately, many people have come to Madonna House; it seems that during this past year they have brought new doubts. This past year they have been asking, "Should one pray? Is there a need for prayer?" At first I thought the question was a joke, but soon discovered that it wasn't. Men and women were seriously discussing this subject and asking themselves, "Should we pray?"

I remembered the scriptural teaching, "Pray always." I remembered how Jesus, rising before daybreak, went out to a desert place, and there he prayed. I remembered the Old Testament prophets who prayed constantly. I thought of all the ordinary, humble people of the world who pray daily—the Mohammedans, the Hindus, the Christians— and, somehow, I became afraid!

The ways of God are really strange and incomprehensible. Some priests are giving up the Breviary, while some laity are picking it up and finding nourishment for their spiritual lives. In many families, husbands and wives recite it with their children. Contemplative monasteries dedicated to prayer are losing members and not getting new vocations. On the other hand, our hermitage-poustinias in Madonna House are filled throughout most of the year. People are hungering for the utter silence and solitude of such places. A strange paradox, to say the least!

Prayer is such a deep need of man. To throw out prayer is to throw out faith. To throw out faith is to deny and throw out God himself. To deny God is to deny the Lord Jesus Christ; it is to enter a loneliness that is the true hell of man. It is a hell of his own making. Having denied God, man's only alternative will be to make himself a god. That means that he will behold himself constantly in a mirror, and is there a greater loneliness than being enclosed in the prison of self, the worship of self?

I suppose it is possible to live without prayer, but it will be a cold, empty life. Why should it be like that? Prayer is a song. Prayer is a tremendous happening between God and man. Prayer is the door to peace. Prayer is the child of faith, but also in a sense its father, because it makes faith grow. Prayer is a physician and a companion. Prayer is the strength of the weak. Prayer moves mountains and changes things. Prayer is humble and meek. Prayer is powerful and strong.

Having said all this, I feel I haven't said anything. My father and mother taught me from childhood to lift two arms to God: prayer and penance. Old-fashioned? Conservative? Perhaps. But millions of people are going to gurus, looking into the spiritual ways of the Eastern religions. Millions are turning their faces, hearts and minds to men and women from distant lands who *pray*. Why this interest in prayer and in these gurus who fast and pray? Evidently, these gurus are not conservative, are not old-fashioned. In fact, they are just the opposite: they are the "in" thing! Only the *Christian* call to prayer seems to be outdated. Why is that?

As I walked across the bridge that leads to my island I prayed that once again those Christians among us who have stopped praying would turn their faces to Christ and say with the apostles, "Lord, teach us how to pray as John taught his disciples."

* * * * * * * * * *

My island is gradually becoming a green cell. Soon I will be sheltered even from the boats that pass so close. They may suspect there is a house on the island, because its roof protrudes above the bushes.

My house cannot be seen in the summer from across the river. Yet, my bridge connects me to the whole world and, what is more astonishing, the world to me.

Do not get the idea that I am a hermit! I may be now and then, for I have a small poustinia a short distance from my cabin where I may pray in total solitude, and where I can fast and weep over the world and my own sins. No, though my island is a green cell, I have but occasional moments of solitude there. My log cabin is my office as well as my living quarters, and I am quite comfortable with old-fashioned ways of living. During most of my stay here I washed my hair and took my bath as our ancestors did— in a basin!

No, I am not a hermit on my island. Far from it. My bridge connects me with the world both by letters and by people constantly coming to visit. Strange, when we first came to Combermere at the request of Bishop William Smith, it was even then a faraway place. It seemed to be a "dead-end street." There was a time when trains came only three times a week to our railroad station 13 miles away. There was no bus service.

Last summer Madonna House had a thousand visitors!

It seems that no matter where the apostles of the world go, sooner or later the world beats a path to their doors. When I was in Harlem in 1938 and 1939 I was told that

only a few white people ever came there. But very soon
hundreds of white people came to visit our Friendship
House. They came from all over New York and from
other states as well, and from Canada. People came from
foreign countries, and not only lay people but prelates and
priests and religious as well.

And so it is now with me at Madonna House and on
my island. Eighteen thousand letters a year come to my
desk here in front of the one big window, from which
I can see my Russian shrine, the river, the forest, the
mountains and the hills.

Shrine, river, forests, hills—all help me to answer
those letters. Some are beautiful and consoling letters.
Some are letters of tortured souls crying in the night. Some
are filled with seemingly unsolvable problems. Some speak
of a soul's search for God. Every letter is a human contact.
Every letter calls for love, understanding, and more love,
peopling my island with my brothers and sisters in Christ
everywhere. No, I'm far from being a hermit!

In the warm months of the year, beginning somewhere
in April and ending somewhere late in October, people
come. They cross the bridge and I can hear voices approaching. Some are sad, some are laughing. As they
enter my green cell they become silent, pleasantly so.
Silent and thoughtful.

Often they go first to the Russian shrine. I can see
them pray quietly before it. I come out of my log cabin to
greet them. I invite them in for a visit, or a talk maybe in
the sun outside if it is warm. There we sit, surrounded by
the red crosses of my Way of the Cross on the pines, and
we talk.

Strange, isn't it, that I roam the world by letters and
prayer, and so many people come to visit me? No, I certainly am no hermit, though I live in a green cell on an
island.

Summer

My island teaches me new truths, or deepens the truths I already know. Like life, the island is never the same. Who of us has not known those "naked days" when we feel the world is against us, that its prying eyes strip us naked and leave us crucified; days when we feel we would give anything for a little privacy; days of sorrow and pain when we want to hide and have no place to hide?

But if one reads the scriptures and comes across its lovely poetic words about a "garden enclosed," a "fountain sealed," and wonders about it all, then my island will reveal the secret of those holy words, and it will lead gently to contemplation, which is the key to that garden. Someday, unseen and unheard, the Bridegroom will come into such a garden. Then one will understand what it is to be all his.

My island now, and for many months, will be trying to teach me about such things. And I am glad. It is so easy to learn from the book of nature, the book of an island made by God about God. I tell my island that I will be waiting. In the meantime, I know that if I listen well, with my soul and my heart, if I fold the wings of my intellect completely, my island will reveal its secrets to me someday!

* * * * * * * * * *

The bond of charity is strong in the Russian soul, placed there not only by the grace of baptism, but by the loving hands of parents, and by the conscience of a whole

people. That is how it was in Russia in the old days. Even
the illiterate peasant realized deeply both the responsibility
and the privilege of a Christian to love, to weep, to atone,
and to pray for all his brethren.

The sun goes down quietly in July, painting the sky
in marvelous colors that take one's breath away. At least
they do mine. And there always comes a moment at eventide when my island is bathed in a sort of golden mist
reflected from the glowing skies. This is the moment I love
very deeply. It reminds me of Pentecost and the fire of the
Holy Spirit. Then I stand before the Holy Trinity, realizing
the miracle of God's love, understanding not with the
intellect alone, but with my whole being, that I have a
Father, that we all have a Father, and that our Father is
God. I realize that Christ our brother became a man, lived
on the earth, died on Golgotha, and rose on the third day to
bring us back to his Father. I realize that the Holy Spirit
is present, shedding his fire in our hearts, illuminating our
minds to plunge into the mysteries of God's love.

Yes, this is the moment I love best of all. This is the
moment when it seems to me that I can lift the world and
hold it as a mother holds a child—lift it up for the Holy
Trinity to bless. This is the moment when I am so free that
I can go a-visiting across the whole world in the twinkling
of an eye. I can visit my brother Trappists and Carmelites
in their enclosures and pray with them and for them.

This is the moment when I can go and ask the blessing
of all the priests I love so much, and for whom I never
cease praying. This is the moment when I can travel to
Asia, Africa, every part of the world, bringing, I hope, the
cool waters of my prayers and love for my brothers and
sisters in Christ everywhere. This is the moment when I am
one with every human being on earth. This is the moment
when I touch the holy souls in Purgatory, the moment when

I speak to the Church Triumphant, to all the saints I love and all the people I know must surely be there.

I call this moment my moment of grace, of joy, a moment in which, through his infinite mercy, God enlarges my heart and allows me to take into it the whole world. I send my prayers upwards to his throne in the golden glow of a setting sun. My island ceases to be a cell. It becomes instead part of an immense, miraculous world of souls.

This is the moment, too, when I understand a little better the essence of the apostolate. I understand what *being before the Lord* means. I understand how important is this inner unity, this fire of charity that seems to grow in my heart and how vital it is for a true apostolate. Yes, this is it! This is the alpha and omega of the apostolate: this opening of oneself to everyone in a simple prayer before an old-fashioned shrine. The shrine, of course, is not necessary. Such an opening can be done anywhere and at all times—and should be. From this all action flows. And if this inner unity, this inner love, this inner constant prayer for the whole world and the Church is not present, then one's apostolate is sterile.

The evenings in July are long. This is the time I come, after a hard day's work, to refresh myself and be refreshed, to pray, to be one with the whole world before the face of my Father who is my God.

*   *   *   *   *   *   *   *   *   *

There is much activity on my island during the summer. Often many young people gather in my cabin to discuss the things that fill their hearts. Sometimes a group of priests and I discuss at length ways and means of enlarging the heart of the world. We discuss the manifold ways and techniques of achieving that enlargement: liturgy, catechetics, scripture, the secular knowledge and technical skills that must be acquired to serve the heart of humanity better. The whole question of missions is often touched upon. Yet, at the end of all these discussions, it is agreed that the only way to enter a heart, to enlarge it, to give it the vision of God, is to cry the gospel with your own life. In other words, the whole apostolate begins with love, continues with love, and leads to love.

Yes, my island and my log cabin are scenes of much exterior activity. But they are also scenes of inner, hidden activity. Perhaps I should call it wrestling with God, with myself, and with the apostolate. Only a person engaged in the apostolate knows the tremendous stress and strain that a human being is subject to when he deals with God and the things of God. Every step of the way brings new decisions to be made. Sometimes quick decisions must be made on the spur of the moment. Sometimes they are long-range decisions that bring me into a wrestling match with God, a struggle like Jacob's with the angel. My mind, soul and heart wrestle with spiritual problems until the body gives up in sheer exhaustion, to rest for a while and then to come alive again and start the wrestling all over again.

The question of training youth, for example, for our type of lay apostolate, is a topic which involves struggling of this kind. Our mission field is the whole world. Our vocation is one of total dedication to the works of the apostolate in the marketplace under promises of poverty, chastity and obedience.

How should we train our young people to go to the ends of the earth? For the very essence of our apostolate is that we are lay people involved in the problems of living, as all lay people are. Young people see the tremendous changes of our restless world, the breaking up of the old patterns, new ones not yet formed. What should be put into the training that will equip one for such a world? That is the constant question that gnaws at all those who, like myself, head such apostolates.

It may seem quite simple: all one has to do is train people to proclaim the glad news of the gospel that God loved us first and that we must love him back! But this must be accomplished in young people who are filled with the remnants of Jansenism, Puritanism, and all the anxieties of our modern world. There is no doubt, however, that the restoration of the world begins with what might be called the "cream of the crop," the leaders among the young. It is they whose hearts must first be enlarged to absorb the tremendous vision of our faith: that life is a love affair between God and man, and not a set of rules to keep.

I have wrestled with this problem for 40 years now, and I am still wrestling with it; I think I shall continue to struggle with it till the day I die. For every day brings new problems to solve, new ideas to absorb, new needs to fill. As I have said, my mail alone brings questions and problems from all parts of the world; each pleads for an answer, a clarification, a word of comfort.

When the night comes, and I behold my green island cell, the contrast between its peace and the world's unrest is so sharp that I can only fall on my knees and pray for the world and for myself, imploring God to give us faith and strength. Pray for me, please. It is not easy to wrestle with the problems of humanity and, at times, with God!

* * * * * * * * * *

I constantly cross my bridge to meet men and women, bishops and priests, rich and poor, sick and healthy. And when I cross over again to the island, they all come back

with me—not in person, not in the flesh, but I carry them
back in my mind and heart. I talk to God about them and
I thank him for having brought them to Madonna House so
that I could hold them and give them room in the inn of
my heart.

Then there are the nights. There are times when I
wake up instantaneously, feeling very refreshed and rested.
These are the moments when, again, the humanity that I
meet in Madonna House, and the brothers and sisters I met
only in the mail, seem to throng onto my island and into my
log cabin.

And the strangest thing happens: both my island and
my log cabin, even as my heart, seem to expand immeasur-
ably so as to accommodate the multitudes. Together we
talk to one another and to God. Yes, there are the nights,
the quiet, starlit, moonlit, overcast nights that make me
one with all the world, but especially with my brothers and
sisters in Christ.

*   *   *   *   *   *   *   *   *   *

It occurred to me today that Mary should be the
patroness of laypeople. Let's face it, she was a laywoman,
lay in the fullest sense of that term. To all eyes she was the
wife of a carpenter, the mother of a son. She was a house-
wife who kept house, sewed, wove. Didn't she weave the
seamless robe of Christ? She must have been a good
weaver. She washed her laundry at the same pool as all the
other village women. In no way was she distinguishable
from the average villager. She lived with her son, a
carpenter, for an indefinite number of years, and was sup-
ported by him.

What better model, what better patroness, what better
helper could ordinary lay folk have than Mary? Shouldn't
we ask her help in times of turmoil, in a world filled with

confusion, anxieties and problems? I think that she must have had a harder time than we do.

One day, out of nowhere, while she was busy with her chores, an angel spoke to her and gave her a fantastic, an incredible message: she would be the mother of the long-awaited Messiah. She accepted this role with simple words, saying that she was ready to do God's will. She said *fiat*.

But that was only the first of 10,000 *fiats* she had to say. She had to say *fiat* during Joseph's bewilderment. She had to say *fiat* when she gave birth in a miraculous fashion to her child. What must have been her thoughts when she resumed her humdrum life? Nothing happened. This child, who was to be the Messiah, was just a boy like any other boy. He ate, slept; his diapers had to be changed. Then he grew up and helped Joseph around the carpentry shop. He learned the trade. Once in a while he "stepped out of line," so to speak, as when he stayed behind in the temple at Jerusalem and caused his parents such grief.

Serenely, silently, Mary accepted all this. But she must have been wondering what it was all about—even as many people today are wondering what it was all about! However, we wonder without her serenity, without her peace, without her love and without her faith and trust. How we need her attitudes and her endlessly repeated *fiats!* She was no ordinary woman, though she might have appeared to be in the eyes of all her neighbors. What courage it took to live like Mary! What faith!

Suddenly, without warning, her son leaves her. He drops everything and goes preaching all over Palestine. She probably heard many rumors about him, and not all of them very flattering! So many accused him! This must not have been her idea of a Messiah either, or was it?

Shouldn't Mary be, then, the patroness of a laity that hears all kinds of rumors about Christ? "Christ is not God." "Christ is only a prophet." "God is dead." "God is alive." She will give us the courage to sort things out in the silence of our hearts. She will help us to grow in faith and in love and to follow her son as she did.

Shouldn't we who believe, who suffer, who are in anguish and anxiety, shouldn't we stand with her under the cross? Shouldn't we find, through her, the courage to keep believing and to stand still while the Church, the Bride of Christ, bleeds from a thousand wounds? Shouldn't we turn to her, who held her son in her arms, in order to find the strength to bear the burdens which tear the souls of Christians apart? If we do turn to her she will lead us to his resurrection and show us the essence of an unshakeable faith.

Wasn't this ordinary Jewish laywoman the strength and the consolation of the apostles before Pentecost? Yes, Mary is a profound mystery of consolation. If we turn to this woman wrapped in silence, she will speak to us. The one through whom God came to us will lead us back to him. She is the Queen of Apostles and Martyrs.

As I sit on my island in the great silence of nature, I give Mary a very simple name: Mother of the People of God. May she teach us how to remain people of faith in a world that cannot recognize her son as the Messiah.

*   *   *   *   *   *   *   *   *   *

Today my mind goes back some 15 years ago when the first bridge to this island was replaced. It was a simple, narrow wooden bridge with that beautiful silver-gray sheen of wood long exposed to sun, rain and snow. If it could speak, it would have spoken of many tales of joy and sorrow. I had walked over it so many times, bent on so many errands.

There was the night I returned from a sickbed—in

fact, the deathbed of a neighbor whom I had nursed. My heart was filled with sorrow at the parting, and I was praying for the repose of his soul as I crossed my bridge. That was the time when Eddie, my husband, was very sick. I had relinquished my log cabin to him because it was quiet, away from the hustle and bustle of Madonna House.

One of our priests met me that night at the far end of my bridge, telling me to hurry, for Eddie had received the last rites! He had had a heart seizure! I ran. That old bridge knew my fears and sorrows that night. But it also knew my joy a few days later when Eddie recovered and we crossed over it, back to the mainland.

My bridge had known the tread of bishops from distant mission lands, and that of saintly visiting priests. It knew the slow steps of tired souls who came to rest at Madonna House. It knew the eager steps of youth who came to join the apostolate and give their lives gallantly to God. Yes, my bridge could tell many stories, sad and funny stories, heroic and humble. But that year it was no more. It died as all things die. I watched the dismantling of it with tears in my eyes and took some pictures to remember it by.

For about a week then I had no bridge. A new one was being built. A nice, sturdy span it turned out to be, wider than the old one, more solidly built. But it took us a while to get acquainted!

During that week I used a boat to get to my island. I felt very isolated at night. The stream that divides the island from the mainland is not very big, so the trip in the boat did not take very long. But somehow I still felt cut off, alone. The line of communication between me and the rest of the world had grown very thin and I began to understand many things that I hadn't understood before.

I understood better the words of God, "It is not good

for man to be alone." I recalled how fear can be born
in the hearts of men when they live apart from other men;
how everything that isn't like them can appear dangerous,
evil and definitely inferior. The mystery of racism became
clearer, and many other things as well.

The death of my bridge taught me much about life,
and I am thankful. It taught me the difference between
collectivism and community. The collective is nothing less
than a caricature, a perversion of community into more
organization, degrading it to the level of mere association.
Genuine community is not constituted simply by pursuits
of common objectives. Nor is it achieved solely by organization. Community has its roots deep in the very nature of
man. Only in community can man attain to the full
measure of individuality and personality. I had read these
ideas in Father Haring's wonderful book, *The Law of
Christ;* the fullness of his thoughts only hit me upon the
death of my bridge.

It was good for me to be without the bridge for a
week! Good to have to travel by boat to and from the mainland. I learned much. I learned in depth that no man can
be an island and call himself a real person. I'm glad I have
a new bridge. It isn't as graceful as my old one, but it will
serve me and others for many years to come.

It will bridge much more than water.

*   *   *   *   *   *   *   *   *   *

As I sit before my lovely large cross I wonder what
has happened to us as human beings. All of us hunger for
the open spaces and the simple life—but few people do
anything about it. As I go lecturing to the busy, crowded
world of cities and suburbs, I hear the cry—like a dirge,
like a dark refrain through some inner, unsung melody—

"Oh, if we could only get out of this rat race and live someplace where it is peaceful, quiet and close to nature."

Yet, before one can really implement this desire, one must begin a pilgrimage of opening one's eyes and unplugging one's ears. This pilgrimage begins with prayer to Christ who made the blind man see and opened the ears of a deaf man. Before you can find peace outside yourself, you must have silence and quiet in your heart and in your mind. Then, when your eyes are opened and your ears are unplugged, you will see the birds that come to perch on your windowsills or on the tiny handkerchief lawn that is in front of your house. Then you will notice the lonely lilac bush that blooms in the yard next door, or in the park. Like St. Francis of Assisi, you will find many little animals and birds to talk to, right where you live. What is more important, you might even learn to listen to them! If you do, I guarantee they will tell you many secrets of God and many secrets about people.

It is wonderful, of course, to get into the open and talk to wild animals, but not everyone can do this. There are birds and animals in the city if only we have the eyes to see and the peace in our hearts to listen. Sometime I will tell you, my friends, what the animals tell me on my island.

* * * * * * * * * *

Here in the natural peace of cool woods and greenery, I try to endure the pain that fills my soul, mind and heart. What is the essence of that pain? The essence of that pain is Christ, whom so many of us are failing. I have witnessed the leadership that belongs to Christians slip from our hands and pass over into the hands of the secular world. There, men follow not the standards of the loving, merciful God, but the standard of mere humanitarianism in which God has almost no part.

We Christians—with a few exceptions—seem to be islands, not bent on sticking our necks out but on protecting ourselves. From what? From whom? From getting involved, it seems to me, in the burning questions of the day, especially the questions of the rights of minority groups. Questions of principle must now be lived in the marketplace, no matter what the cost. Yet, we prefer to remain little islands, minding our own business, never making bridges between us and others.

The pain in my heart grows bigger. I didn't think it could. But my island—its beauty and the reflection of God's face it portrays—gives me the strength to put down bridges in all directions, bridges of prayer, fasting and penance.

The vigil light, lit at sunset before my Russian shrine, glows like a jewel in the dark when I return to my island from the mainland. It is before this shrine that I kneel in the quiet of a summer night. I beseech the Mother of God, our Lady of Kiev, our Lady of Russia, to save her children the world over, save them from the catacombs into which so many of us are headed. We may be leading the Church into those catacombs through our noninvolvement, our noncommitment, through our remaining islands without bridges.

What else, I ask our Lady, can I do? Only what I am already doing? The apostolate of Madonna House grows and gets involved in every phase of Canadian-American life where involvement is needed. But that is not enough. Nor is it enough simply to raise one's voice in print and through lectures. "Stand firm as we do and don't be moved," say the trees. "Cease not to pray like we do," whisper the grass and the flowers. "Continue to weep over the sins of mankind," sings the river as she passes by my island.

There is always an answer to be found. I thank God for giving me such a wise island which allows my pain to remain and counsels me how to assuage the pain of Christ.

*   *   *   *   *   *   *   *   *   *

There are moments in one's life when time stops. I experienced such a moment a few years ago when Archbishop Raya, who was then Father Raya, pastor of a Melkite parish in Birmingham, Alabama, brought two large icons of Our Lord and Our Lady to Madonna House. The occasion was the ordination jubilee of one of our priests, Father Briere. It happened during supper, and there were about a hundred people in the dining room.

The icons were so big that Father Raya and a young man who came with him were completely hidden behind them. All I saw was Christ and his Blessed Mother walking through the door!

Time stopped! I couldn't breathe. I sat like a statue, unmoving. Perhaps I should say that time reversed itself. For here, in our little town of Combermere, the Christ of Russia and his Mother, the *Bogoroditza* (the Russian name for Our Lady), literally walked toward me in the presence of those icons.

I had a flashback. In a second I was back in my homeland, and tears were welling up in my eyes. A lifetime passed before me. Memories crowded, flooded, in. I saw and heard once again the people of God in Russia freely filling the churches and singing their beautiful chants, glorifying God and Mary.

Then Father Raya came forth, and the icons were put in our chapel upstairs. I spent quite a little bit of time in the chapel that evening; I spent more time awake in my island cabin. There was no denying it: I was utterly and completely overwhelmed by the goodness of God and of Our Lady.

For well nigh 40 years now I have been asking myself why I, a refugee from Russia and from Communism, a stranger in this new land which I love so much, why should I be chosen by God to found a lay apostolate? Throughout this vast continent there were many people who obviously could have done a better job. Many answers have been suggested to me over the years by holy priests and prelates. Some have said, and rightly so, that God chooses the weakest, the poorest, so that his glory can better shine through. But that night the icons came, I finally got my answer.

God might have chosen a Russian in order to bring to this land a little bit of our simplicity, of our contemplative spirit, of our passivity. Perhaps he just wanted a humble bridge between the Latin and Eastern rites, for in Russia I was brought up in both the Latin and Eastern rites. I was Polish and Russian, with an Orthodox mother and a Catholic father. From early babyhood I had been steeped in both and have absorbed them both, as it were.

Now, there at Madonna House, was the Lord Christ of Russia and his Mother, the *Bogoroditza,* coming into our chapel. These icons were especially dedicated to the re-union of East and West. They were installed, blessing the Western world in an Eastern way, bringing about by their very presence a unity based on love, on prayer and on understanding of one another's traditions.

For 35 years I have been trying to work and pray for the unity of the Eastern and Western churches. At the beginning of the Council we built a Russian shrine. A vigil light burned before the icon of Our Lady for the deliberations of the Council. And all during the years of the Council meetings there was a Latin shrine facing the

Russian one. On my island the two Churches were already blending into one.

Perhaps I have exaggerated a point or two here, but all I know is that all that night after the arrival of those two icons, my heart was filled with a gratitude to Jesus Christ that was beyond expression. May the name of the Lord be glorified forever—at Madonna House and everywhere else! Truly his love, his mercy and compassion are infinite and everlasting. Alleluia!

* * * * * * * * * *

The other day I was reading a French magazine published in Paris by the Teilhard de Chardin Circle. As I was reading the brilliant analysis of this priest there suddenly came to mind the picture of an old Russian woman pilgrim. She had come to our house when I was a child and had talked to me while I served her food in the warm kitchen of our big country house.

She told me about the joy of being a pilgrim, of walking on green grass and stopping to rest at a tree trunk. She said an old tree trunk had so many colors. Did I think a birch was white? No, she said, it wasn't white. It had black spots all over it. The white of the bark had many shades. One has only to look at it closely to know. And the same with pines and oaks. Tree barks were a symphony of color.

And the green of the forest, she said, is of a thousand hues. As she was speaking I could see all that she said actually taking shape before my eyes, for I loved nature, too. But, she went on to explain, this quality of wonderment, of joy and of appreciation had to be a prayer, because of God. It was God who had created all this beauty. He, the humble carpenter of Nazareth, was, as she put it, the king of the trees and the stars and the earth and the moon,

king of the tiniest blade of grass, of every insect that ever
lived, of all the animals, and especially, of course, of
people. All these creatures were in God and he was in us.

I put down the Teilhard de Chardin magazine and
picked up a book I had just recently received, *Russian Piety*
by Nicholas Arseniev. He was quoting a Russian peasant
woman also. There I read once more the same words that
the pilgrim of my childhood had spoken to me. And here
they are:

> When we left our village and looked about
> us—Lord, it seemed to us that God's world had
> no end or limit. What divine grace shines on
> high in the heavenly places! And down under-
> foot, here is the green grass, and the golden corn;
> and over there is the forest, almost too thick,
> you'd think, to pass through. When you walk in
> silence, or rest on the ground, you think you are
> hearing a constant chanting, full of gentleness.
> Everything is humming and gurgling, dripping
> and murmuring around you, as if the Lord him-
> self were speaking to you through the mouth of
> all creation.

Teilhard de Chardin, the modern genius, and these
two old Russian peasant women, met on my island today,
and once more I understood that both were truly childlike.
It is to such childlike ones that the Lord reveals the
mysteries of his kingdom.

*   *   *   *   *   *   *   *   *   *

Once again the sparkling sun is reflected in the blue
Madawaska, and I have been thinking, of all things, about
confession! Lately, it seems to me, Catholics have talked
a lot about confession. I have read quite a few articles

about it, too, and I'm thinking how strange it all is.

Due to my Russian heritage, I have always considered confession a wonderful thing. When I was little, it meant going to a church, kneeling before a priest, and telling him my thoughts. In my imagination it was much more than that, however. My mother, very gently and simply, explained it. I had committed a fault and knew that God wouldn't like it, so I sort of ran towards him and, sitting on his lap and putting my arms around his neck, I would kiss him—like I did my father—and tell him how sorry I was for having done something he didn't like.

In my imagination, Christ hugged me and said something like, "That's all right, little girl. I know it is not easy to always do the right thing." Then he would kiss me and bless me and say, "Now go and play."

Yes, confession is Christ's kiss of peace, of forgiveness. It's a simple thing, not very complicated. Perhaps the way my mother taught me stayed with me. I was never afraid to go "in the box" (or "out of the box," as I often had to do in rural parishes). Always, before my eyes, were the love and forgiveness of God, and his immense mercy.

Confession was never a place, nor even a priest. I never looked at the priest, for clearly, I always saw Christ. Confession was always a joy. I was never taught to go to confession on a certain date or at a certain time. I knew that I had to go to confession once a year at least. That seemed pretty funny. Surely one would like to go and be blessed by Christ and hear his words, "Go in peace," more than once a year! Thus, I went when the Spirit moved me. Sometimes I would go every day for a week or two or more. Then I would say to Christ, "By your grace, I haven't committed any sins or faults that I know of, but I am very weary and tired so I come to get your kiss of peace and be covered with the mantle of your mercy once again; I need it so much for tomorrow."

So I was wondering what all those discussions about confession were about. All kinds of arguments are brought forth in those articles—arguments about the dangers of legalism, about the fear that surrounded the sacrament in the past, and how, because of these things, it must be changed. I think what should be changed is not the confessional box, nor the practice of open confession such as the Russians have and which is now frequently the practice in parishes. No. I think the change must come through the hearts of men.

The change must come from the parents who are the primary teachers of the spiritual life of their children. It must come from parents whose own consciences are delicately formed, and who can transmit that delicacy to their children. From the parents, the child absorbs the power to distinguish between good and evil, the ability to examine his or her conscience openly and in peace; from the parents the child acquires the understanding of Christ's infinite mercy and love.

Didn't Christ say, "I have come not for those who are healthy, but for the sick, and not for the just, but for sinners"? He spoke of himself as a physician, a healer. So what is all this talk about confession? Who of us would not mind standing in line before a doctor's office if he or she were sick? Do we really mind standing in line to be kissed by Christ?

For those of us who have been guided by our parents, it seems rather incomprehensible that so much fuss should be raised about going to confession. A sick person goes to a doctor; so a childlike soul goes to Christ to be consoled, to be healed, to be forgiven. It is like a lover running into the arms of the Beloved.

*   *   *   *   *   *   *   *   *   *

As I cross my bridge every day, I meet frogs! They remind me of the many bullies I know, and of little people who try to be important. These frogs of mine can really blow themselves up to strange and immense sizes. They do not realize that the more they blow themselves up, the uglier they look. I watch them bully the little frogs as some people bully others. Having bullied them a long time, they then push them around. They (the frogs!) often end up by eating the little guys. Doesn't this likewise often happen among people? There are thousands of ways of eating and swallowing a human being.

I watch the beautiful dragonfly covering my bridge with the beauty of its colorful wings. But I also note that this beauty is short-lived. It makes me meditate constantly on the shortness of life and question whether *I* bring beauty into it, the supreme beauty that alone is lasting forever and ever—the beauty of God's love.

There are water snakes in my marshes that I can watch if I stand quietly without moving. They come from nowhere and swim silently back to nowhere, blending with the water lilies and the other vegetation that grow in marshy places. It is fascinating to watch them approach their prey. They do not pounce on it as some in the animal kingdom do. They shorten their swimming rounds, circling around their prey in ever-decreasing circles, seeming to hypnotize their victims by some kind of whispering. The prey, immobilized, watches them, fascinated, unaware that death is closing in.

The eternally repeated story in man's life of the tree and the apple, of the serpent, the man, and the woman, comes vividly before me. As I watch my water snakes I find myself with tears in my eyes when finally the snake gets its prey. For I think of the millions of men and women who, like this prey, could have escaped, jumped away, if only they had not been fascinated by danger and knew the truth which is God.

I've been meaning to explain to you how I obtained the Stations of the Cross on my island. One year I prayed to the Lord about them. I prayed because our men are very busy and cannot spend time making 14 crosses to put on trees! I have always loved the Way of the Cross and I wanted to pray it quietly on my island, which lends itself so well to meditation and contemplation.

Time went by. One day, 14 little crosses arrived as, quite frankly, I had expected them to! These I had painted red. They are all nailed to pine and birch trees across my island, and I can pray the stations in peace in this natural cathedral of God.

My island does resemble a little cathedral. The pines are old, and so are the birches. They make a canopy out of their branches that is beautiful to behold. Green bushes and little trees make up the walls. And soft pine needles, brown with golden flecks, make the floor, through which, here and there, wild flowers and colorful mushrooms grow. I walk from tree to tree, from station to station, praying for all those whom I love, for all those who love me, and for all those who do not love me. But, especially, I pray for the world and for all men that they may come to know and love God.

It is a blessing to see a little cross on a big tree. It brings you closer to Christ whose cross was fashioned out of a living green tree. As I wend my way beneath the canopy of branches which are shot through with vivid patches of sun and dark shadows, I realize that an island is an image of two things: the bridge between God and man, and the place where, alone, man meets God. In order to be able to build bridges among men and walk across them, one must first enter the garden enclosed and meet the God who dwells there.

* * * * * * * * * *

The animals tell me things when I am very quiet and sit very still on one of my red lawn chairs. (I love red. It makes me think of the Holy Spirit whom we in Russia call the Crimson Dove, the God of love.)

I want you to understand clearly that it takes a while for animals to "size somebody up." They are very shrewd. They know many things which are hidden from our eyes—things about man himself, even though they are inferior to him. When they look at him they see the image of their Creator. Obviously, they know that man is different. Another thing that matters very much is that one should have the peace of the Lord in one's heart. Animals know somehow, it seems to me, when there is unpeace in our hearts, distorting this image of the Creator.

So don't try to approach animals when you are unpeaceful, angry or disturbed. If you are peaceful and ready to sit for a while and look around you with eyes and ears that really see and hear, a little squirrel will eventually peep out from behind the white front of a birch and survey you from a distance. Then, slowly, it will start running circles around you, as if it were looking over the terrain for pinecones or nuts. Keep still. The animals are really reconnoitering you. Let them run around and hide and come out again and again. Be still when they come closer and closer.

That's what happened with my two squirrels. A wooden statue couldn't have been more still than I was when they finally approached very close. They settled themselves on their haunches and then they began talking to each other and talking to me. Occasionally, they interrupted each other to correct some exaggeration, I guess, or to fill some gap in the narrative.

And this is the story they told me.

They had heard that ancestors of theirs had lived in Palestine and that there had been a place in Kedron where very special cedars grew. These cedars had very special little brown nuts that were just what a squirrel liked. There were groves and groves of these cedars, and they bordered fields of a poor man and a rich man who both loved squirrels and let them eat all the nuts they desired.

One day a rich man—and very fat he was—came to visit the poor man who owed the rich man a lot of money. The rich man threw the poor man out of his field and out of his home. Wanting to enlarge the field, the rich man ordered his men to cut down all the cedars. Disaster threatened the food supply of the squirrels.

Sure enough, the day came when all the cedars were cut down. All the squirrels gathered on the poor man's property. Suddenly, a man came walking through the field towards them. They weren't afraid of him at all. They stopped their crying but didn't scatter. The man spoke to them. They loved the sound of his voice. He asked them what had happened. They told him. He lifted his arms and made a strange sign over the place where the cedars had been. And right before their very eyes the cedars were back again, growing and laden with fruit even more than before. It was incredible!

At that moment the fat rich man came waddling along. He upbraided the visitor. The eyes of the good man darkened and his voice became as a voice of thunder as he told the fat man that he who defrauds the poor defrauds and mocks God. The fat man was frightened and ran away. But he ran too fast. He had a heart attack and died right there in the dust of the road.

That ended the first part of the story. But the squirrels heard that the ousted poor man had received an inheritance from someplace and redeemed his field. The ancestors of my squirrels swore by all that is holy that the name of the man who made the cedars grow again was Jesus, and that in him they saw God as clearly as they had ever seen him. There was no doubt about it. And it is said to this day that any squirrel who eats of the cedar nuts of Kedron will be especially blessed.

My squirrels told me that each year, from each country and each squirrel tribe, an elder goes to make the pilgrimage. They have learned to share their nuts with all the poor squirrels, the sick squirrels. They want to know why men don't also do this since God told them to.

At this point, as I tried to explain it to them, I moved slightly, and my squirrels scampered away. But they came back again. I'll tell you perhaps some other time how the conversation continued. You can learn strange things from the wild animals if you sit quietly and have peace in your heart!

* * * * * * * * * *

The quiet and silence of my island was shattered joyfully one summer when Madonna House experienced one of the largest summer school attendances since 1949, the year of our first school of 10 students. The summer of which I am now speaking was the 14th, and the first time we did not have enough beds for everyone. We had to accommodate some of our young people in sleeping bags on the stage of our new theater in the basement of St. Germaine's. This new house had been built to take care of the increasing numbers of young people who kept coming for such summer schools. But it wasn't big enough! Some even had to sleep in their cars that summer. But it was fun. We loved to play host to them since they had come seeking God and the things of God.

All these visitors prayed at my Russian shrine. My island and I were glad to note that so many people knew so much about Eastern rites, Eastern churches, and also about our Protestant and Jewish brothers and sisters. It seemed to me that all nature rejoiced at this. Even the little squirrels and other animals became more friendly as the days went by. Maybe this growing mutual charity in the hearts of the visitors was sensed by the animal kingdom.

The unity and reunion of all peoples truly depends on the love that is in the heart of each one of us towards the other. Ceaselessly I pray that this love may grow, for it alone is the true bridge among us. We may study our differences and learnedly discuss the ways to lessen them. We may become experts in Eastern theology, Protestant beliefs and Roman Catholic doctrine. But if we have no love in our hearts, we shall not be able to foster any unity. Unity is simply the visible sign of love.

Yes, let us begin to love our neighbors whoever they are, and then we shall get to know them because we love them. Love is also a way of knowing and "getting to know." Through such love all people will see the truth that is God.

*   *   *   *   *   *   *   *   *   *

Madonna House is truly a strange place to which, in a sense, the world comes. The main house has five doors, and from hour to hour we never know who will enter through any one of them into our hearts. An avalanche—a beautiful, joyous, avalanche of youth—has been coming this summer to Madonna House. They are boys and girls giving of their time and talents to the work of our apostolate.

They work on the farm, in our rural apostolate at St. Joseph's House, and in our main training center, sharing our life of work and prayer. They enliven our discussions, dialogues and seminars. They give as well as receive from us. They may be the new breed upon whom so many adults look slightly askance, but to us they are the hope of the future—and the joy of today.

Many of them worked on recreation projects with the children of our valley. The trees often hide these small farms and villages from the eyes of passing tourists. Others worked on our farm. The farm enables us to open our doors wide to all who want to come to Madonna House. Without it, we couldn't feed the hundreds who pass through our home every year.

That summer we gathered a ton of strawberries! Now that seems almost unbelievable, but when 100 or so people sit down to a meal, strawberries melt like ice beneath a summer sun!

The young people marvel that our farm kitchen bakes 100 loaves of bread a day. These also disappear as fast as we make them. It is good homemade bread. We also make our own butter and cheese, and of course we have our own milk and cream.

There are also 14 acres of truck gardening. Each year we consume about six tons of potatoes, a ton of carrots, a ton of turnips, a half-ton of beets and parsnips, not to mention hundreds of heads of cabbage which end up as sauerkraut in the fall. We freeze much swiss chard (which takes the place of spinach), red currants, black currants and gooseberries. All these are grown on the farm. We also make our own apple juice with apples from our own orchards and from some of the orchards in the surrounding countryside. One year we made 600 gallons! And then, of course, there is always the hay for the cows.

It is wonderful to see the joy and eagerness of our young guests as they enter into this manual labor. They realize that the food they are now eating came from the labor of people the summer before, and that their present labor will provide food for those coming next year. But the real fruits of our days cannot be measured, weighed or counted in terms of quantity. For we have really only one goal, one thirst and one desire: to be a community of love.

A community of love must be open to all who knock at its doors. It must be a community aware of the fact that charity, hospitality and availability are the visible signs of its own internal life—signs of its thirst, its hunger for God and its love for one another. Madonna House doesn't believe really in advertising itself, as such. We believe in sharing with others what the Lord has done for us, which is the purpose of the books that have come from Madonna House recently. Once in a while someone "writes us up." We have some literature we send to those who ask for information. Sometimes a magazine will allow us to speak of our needs and our program.

Sometimes, as God's instrument in founding this apostolate, I wonder as to *why* all these people come to the backwoods of Canada. But I have never quite understood. True, we have seminars and discussions about the things of God. But it seems that our guests find something more than words here, something impossible to put into words. They are nourished by just living in Madonna House and being part of our family, our community of love. Though none of us can really explain that, we thank God for it and for being able to share it with others.

As I sit on my island during my few free hours, I thank God again and again for bringing so many people to us. It gets hectic sometimes, and we are tempted to wish the numbers would decrease, but the stranger of a moment ago becomes, in a matter of hours, a deeply beloved friend. No price is too high to pay for that. I am deeply cognizant also that in each person, Christ himself comes to meet us.

My bridge joins me with all the youth of the world, but also with the others that came this summer to Madonna House. It joins me to the hundreds of priests who came in a steady stream. Our priest guest house has been in constant use. Priests come to learn about our apostolate. They come to rest awhile in the gentle hills and quiet countryside that surround us. They come for retreats, to share their troubles with us, their joys and their pains. Through these priests who have come as pilgrims I am joined in a special way with all the priests of the world.

Nuns also come from various religious orders to find answers and also to share answers they have already found. They come to meet the youth of today in an informal atmosphere, conducive to a real meeting of persons. They come to see a lay apostolate in action, and to rest and be refreshed. Through them I am also joined to all the nuns of the world whom I love so much.

Yes, all these people come to Madonna House, and my bridge of love leads me to them and to the Lord. God, in his infinite mercy, enlarges our hearts in Madonna House and fulfills our burning desires to be nothing more— but nothing less—than a community of love to which all men can come to experience God. That is all we, in our poverty, can give or be.

*   *   *   *   *   *   *   *   *   *

In 1970 my island became bigger, that is to say, the part we owned became bigger. We were able at that time to acquire most of it. Perhaps I should go back a little ways. Originally what we owned was a very small part of a larger island, I would say a little less than an acre. The rest of the island belonged to someone else. Down through the years we gradually acquired more and more until in 1970 we owned about 22 acres of it.

At first, I wondered myself why we acquired it. Believe me, a lot of prayers went into that decision. But the growth of the island was another dream I dreamt in the Lord, a dream that suddenly caught up with me and became a reality—but rather unexpectedly, for God's ways are not our ways.

I say "unexpectedly," and yet that isn't quite true. Long ago and far away, between the years 1928 and 1930, I began to dream a dream in the Lord. "Dreaming a dream in the Lord" is sort of the Russian way of talking about one's vocation. I desired very much, as so many of you know, to fulfill God's invitation to the young man, "Sell all you possess, give it to the poor, and come and follow me."

I finally got permission to do so from Archbishop Neil McNeil of Toronto. I sold all that I possessed and, with $15, turned my face toward the poor. I proposed to live in the slums of Toronto, in a little room somewhere, and pray and serve the wretched in humble ways known only to them. I saw my vocation, my dream, as living in a poustinia. In this poustinia of mine I would fast and pray and serve my brothers and sisters in Christ in simplicity and hiddenness.

The Lord had other ideas! In less than six weeks, two men and three young women came and wanted to join me. Frankly, I didn't anticipate this possibility. Everything in me cried out that I wanted to serve God and man alone, according to the ways of my people. They call it "going to the people," as each summer my mother would "go to the people" by hiring herself out to work for the poor in simple ways.

I went to see the archbishop to explain what *my* dream in God was. He smiled, and told me that I should accept these five people. God had chosen me, he said, to be the foundress, the leader, call it what you will, of a lay apostolate. In those days I hadn't heard of the lay apostolate, and I certainly didn't want to be a leader! But my father had told me that a bishop has the fullness of the powers of Christ and his charisms, and that in spiritual matters I should always take my problems to the bishop and obey him.

So I did.

When I was living by myself I used to go with an eight-quart basket and beg my daily food at various shops. They used to give me potatoes, some of which were black-spotted. I used to cut out the spots and have very good potato soup, potato pancakes, potato everything! The lettuce or cabbage might also be bad on the outside, but the inside was still good. Some bakeries gave me bread. Shops often gave me a can of coffee, or half a pound of tea. Plenty for my daily needs.

But now, with five more people to care for, what could I do? Where could I house them? The archbishop suggested that I should give each of them an eleven-quart basket to take out! As for housing, I should beg for it. It was Depression time, and rooms were very cheap. That was the start of Madonna House, then called Friendship House, many years ago.

Today, we have Canadian and American missions, a mission in the West Indies in Carriacou, and this large training center in Combermere, Ontario. The words of the bishop came true: I was indeed to become the foundress of a lay apostolate.

My dream, however, dreamt in the Lord at the beginning of my apostolate, had not vanished. It seems now as if I had simply wrapped it up carefully and put it into my heart. Then, a few years ago, it flamed up again, like a fire that had been burning low in a fireplace. There was a breath of inspiration from the Spirit and it flared up and became a bonfire in my heart.

I've taken this roundabout way of telling you why we finally decided to acquire these 22 acres of my island because, by the grace of God, I had embarked on another foundation! This time it was not a foreign mission. It was a profound entry into the life of prayer. My large island was about to become the home of those who desired to dedicate their lives to prayer in the poustinia.

True, everyone prays at Madonna House, but the poustinia was to be a sort of setting oneself apart for that purpose. And what was so joyous was that there were several of us. Other log cabins were built, making a total of five. (I have another small cabin where I had been praying for quite a while.) Also planned, and now a reality, was a chapel made from logs collected from old barns, woodsheds and such, some almost 100 years old.

These other cabins were designed for three other women to live on the island besides myself, and again, the Russian or Eastern accent was the plan. All of us would spend about three days (maybe four), of each week in silence, prayer and fasting. The rest of the week we would go to the mainland to serve the community in whatever way our services would be needed. As is the custom with the Russian *poustinikki* (hermits), there were to be no latches on our doors: we would be available to anyone who desired to come to us, pray with us, talk about whatever troubled them or made them joyful. A Russian hermit is open to all the sorrows and joys of the world. He prays for everyone who comes, whether they ask for his prayers or not.

Five log cabins and one chapel looked very small on a big 22-acre island, but I believed that others would join us in this life of prayer and service. Yes, in God's own time, they *did* join us. Perhaps, in the not too distant future, the island will be dotted with many log cabins, and East and West will meet on an island in the backwoods of Canada.

God willing, this simple, humble life of prayer and service will help to bring forth a deeper unity in the Church. Who can tell? We are eternally in the presence of the mystery of the mustard seed, the tiny movements of the Spirit which grow and grow.

Those who enter the poustinia must always remember the vertical descent of Christ from the Father, then his horizontal life as man, and his vertical ascent to the Father after his resurrection. This is the pattern for the type of life in the poustinia. Christ emptied himself when he descended from the Father. So too, because of our love for him, we want to empty ourselves so that he may grow to his fullness within us. Someday we may dare to say even as St. Paul, "I live now, not I, but Christ lives in me."

But we must also imitate and identify ourselves with Christ's life as man: he came to wash the feet of man, heal bodies and souls, pray, console others. If we live thus, we too shall rise to the Father after our deaths. During life, we come closer and closer to Christ by living this life—his life—of love, prayer, service and unity.

Fall

The green wall of bushes and trees that surrounds my island is slowly turning golden yellow and various shades of red. The nights are cool. Maybe in the early hours of the morning there is a little frost that as yet gently plays court to each bush and tree, kissing their leaves shyly, without passion. A few more weeks and it will get bolder and the trees and bushes will blush in all their crimson beauty. I watch this transformation with humility, for it teaches me a deep spiritual lesson about liking and loving.

At the springtime of the soul's conversion, when it suddenly realizes that God has loved it first, it desires, with all the flaming desire of youth, to love him back. Like the leaves in the spring, the tender green of the soul sings of innocence and of zeal. Its budding flowers speak of its desire for action and of its great deeds for the Beloved.

Then comes the summertime. Life has brought dust onto the green leaves and toughened them somewhat. The flowers are forming themselves into fruits and seeds—a painful process. So with the soul. Now there is less desire for action. There is more stillness, more recollection, more travail, more pain. But, like the trees and bushes and all living things, the soul continues to serve her Lord faithfully.

With the fall come frequent rains and storms that tear some leaves away. In the autumn of the soul, the

71

storms of life bring many wounds and many scars. The nights get longer and darker. Now the soul walks in faith and sees more clearly; now it begins to know the price of true love. Now it knows that to love God means to enter into the passion of his Son's death, so as to rise with him again.

Frost. It is deadly. It brings death to the leaves, yet it also clothes them in a glory and a beauty that surpass human words. The autumn of the soul is a time for dressing up in the glory of a love that has come to fruition; it is a time for the soul to make herself beautiful for the Lord. Soon, the Angel of Death will bring her the joyful invitation to the wedding with her Beloved. For this she must be prepared. For this her bridal garment must be ready.

This bridal garment will be like Joseph's coat of many colors. There will be gold in it, the gold which the soul brought to the Infant Christ in the springtime of her life. There will be crimson in it, representing the blood she has shed from the many wounds received. There will be green, signifying the hope that never left her; and there will be the white of humility, of chastity, the white also of childlikeness which the loving soul preserved throughout her life. All of these colors—except the white—will be of many shades, and will be exceedingly beautiful.

The whole garment will smell of frankincense, the frankincense of an ever-growing love of God. It will also smell of myrrh, the myrrh of pain and sacrifice.

As I look at all these changing autumn hues, my meditations grow deeper and deeper. For I too am busy preparing my wedding garment!

*   *   *   *   *   *   *   *   *   *

The autumn nights are cold in Combermere. The mists and the fog are not dense. They permit the silhouettes of the mountains and the trees to be seen. Their beautiful outlines covered with a silver veil, they stand clothed in a new beauty which the quiet waters of the river reflect perfectly. Beholding this beauty, my heart bursts out in the one song of gratitude that man has used from time immemorial: Alleluia, alleluia, alleluia!

I think of the subject of vocation, strangely enough, during these beautiful autumn nights on my island. Why? Because vocations are lived in the silvery fog, the beautiful mists of faith. The veil can become thicker or thinner, depending on the person. Prayer thins out the fog and turns it rather into transparent silver curtains that allow us to see the outline, however dimly, of the new Jerusalem, the new Zion, the City of God.

Vocations, those special calls of God to men and women to embrace a definite state in life, are a mystery; yes, a mystery like all the things of God. They are mysteries of love and faith. Our hearts yearn, our minds desire, and our souls hunger for some definite and clear answer about our vocations. We would like to have a letter, personally signed by the Lord himself, telling us that he wants us in this vocation or that!

But God's will and his love are indeed mysterious. He will not speak that clearly. Perhaps the Song of Songs expresses it best: "He draws me with the fragrance of his ointments"; in other words, he draws us by his love. Our vocation is an act of faith and love in him. It is an entry into the silvery night, like my autumn nights in Combermere.

Suddenly he is there, calling us to arise and walk into that mist of faith. It is illuminated by his own light, a thing of joy and beauty, but demanding faith and courage, trust and confidence in him. Such is the life of faith. If only we can get to the bridge of love, and look at it as I am able to look at the beauty of this silvery night! How simple, warm, friendly, beautiful, then, our vocation would be!

We know in faith that he is there with us. We shouldn't be afraid. Temptations will come, but the strength of faith will make them clear to us, and we will walk away from them with firm steps into the beauty of the Lord's will. Our life of faith should be like this indescribable beauty that surrounds my island on these cold autumn nights in Combermere.

*   *   *   *   *   *   *   *   *   *

Why is my heart so heavy today? Why is my soul sad? Why can't I sleep during these cool, lovely nights when the heavens are filled with stars? I ask myself that question and a thousand and one replies crowd into my mind. One reason is that I feel so small, so insignificant, and my poverty as a creature stands before me in all its nakedness. Also, I feel intensely that I am a pilgrim on this earth. The nights, especially, make me realize that I am a pilgrim of the Absolute, one who has arisen in her youth and gone in search of God. According to the ways of my people, God is found in men. I have sought him, consequently, through the apostolate of Madonna House.

Russian pilgrims make their pilgrimages on foot, and there are long stretches when they walk alone. They must often walk through forests and fields, without meeting another human being. It is in the night, here in Canada in the new world, when I understand that this is the hour of *my* walking alone.

It is also the hour of my passion. Every Christian, at one time or another, must enter in a very special and particular way into the passion of Christ. For me, this is the hour, this is the time. This is the moment when the darkness is rent, letting me see the world and its pain, the hatred of brother against brother, nation against nation. God is not only not loved in this world of ours, he is not even known. And where he is known, he is forgotten. To millions upon millions, he does not matter at all, does not exist. Untold other millions set themselves to eradicate him from the minds and hearts of men.

Vividly, the dark night brings these strange sights to the eyes of my soul. In this vision I am truly alone in an agony that staggers the imagination—in a passion that cannot be articulated but simply has to be endured. At these times it seems to me that I am a pilgrim on a thousand different roads, burdened under the weight of a cross I cannot see. However, I can feel, smell and taste the dust. I imagine the Lord also tasted the dust on his way to Golgotha.

*   *   *   *   *   *   *   *   *   *

Have you ever talked to a river? As with the animals, it has to be done very quietly and gently, as well as reverently. The best time is the evening, just before the sun goes down. It seems that the river gets into a reminiscent mood at eventide. At least, mine does. Once she told me all about a canoe that came, it seemed, from the south, bearing three men dressed in black. One was very tall and was using the paddle very gently, without cutting into her waters too deeply. He didn't seem to be in a hurry so that he could take in both her own beauty and that of her shores.

Many a canoe had travelled over her, she said, for she was the highway of the Algonquin tribe of Indians who had lived here long before the white man. She knew these Indians very well and they knew her and all her secrets. But this canoe and these people were different. It wasn't that the color of their skin was different; it was something else

that made her feel both uneasy and glad at the same time.
Something about them made her think of him who had
created her. She told me—my river did—that she couldn't
explain this feeling, but she was truly glad to experience
the weight of that canoe and of these three men all dressed
in black.

They stopped, she said, right opposite my island, on a
flat piece of ground nestling against a lovely green hill.
They must have guessed it was the meeting place of the
Algonquins, for that is where the Indians used to gather for
a powwow after their hunting and fishing.

The men unloaded their canoe, lit a fire and started
to talk. She had never heard words like theirs, but they
fell on her, she said, like a soothing benediction. Later
she found out they had been praying, but at first she was
not sure what had been happening. Whatever it was, it
was lovely!

Then the Indians came. They were as astonished as
she was. But they were glad when the tall one began speaking in their own language.

The meeting of the blackrobes and the Indians lasted
three days. At the end, a most extraordinary thing happened. A young woman and a young brave stepped for-
ward and spoke to the tall man dressed in black. His face
lit up with great joy. He went to the river and took out a
bucket of water. After pronouncing some strange words, he
poured the water over the heads of the two young people.
My river rejoiced that part of her was used in that lovely
ceremony which in later years she found out was called
baptism.

The Indians went their way. The three men in black
entered their canoe once again and returned whence they
had come, traveling slowly again over her waters. The tall
one did a strange thing before leaving. He took a little

cross with a figure of a man on it and dropped it into her depths, and then he made a large Sign of the Cross over her.

At this point in the conversation my river fell silent for a spell. Then, in a low voice, she said: "I was changed that day. My waters became holy. Love had come to dwell within me forever. I had been blessed by him who had made me. I really earned my name that day, Madawaska. It means the 'Beautiful One.' I became beautiful with a beauty I had never known before. Since then, I praise God all the time as I flow my way from north to south. I have taught my riverbanks to do likewise, your island included."

I sat for a long time on the brown earth, my back against a white birch. I knew that my river had told me a story of the first Jesuit martyrs. According to a local legend, Jean Brebeuf and his companions used the Madawaska River as a water route in their travels to the Indians. It is true that the ground on which our parochial school stands was at one time a meeting place for the Indians. From time immemorial, the hill against which the local parish church (which is called The Canadian Martyrs) was built has been called "The Holy Hill."

I rejoiced that I live on an island that may have known their footprints in the days of long ago. It isn't everybody who has the privilege and joy of living in such a hallowed spot.

Be sure, dear friends, if you are traveling, or if you live near a lake or a river, some eventide go and sit by it, especially in those days approaching winter when the waters are quiet. Ask it to tell you some story out of its past. Who knows, but you will find out that you are on hallowed ground. Waters and earth have much to tell us, much to teach us, if we ask them gently, reverently, lovingly.

* * * * * * * * * *

Suddenly I'm back in Harlem, where I had spent so many years of my life in the Friendship House apostolate. I am back in the slums of New York and Toronto and many other cities. The pain of the Negro is again my pain. The hunger of the poor everywhere is my hunger. I hold in my arms the Christ that the atheist killed in the soul of a child. My heart is the inn to which I bring the wounded Christ, wounded by the forgetfulness and the indifference of those he died to save, those he loves so passionately.

My island of splendor, color and beauty suddenly becomes a hill, and it seems as if I am crucified on some tall pine amidst this glory. Suddenly I understand that pilgrims of the Absolute, especially Russian pilgrims, can do more by hanging on some tree for the love of the Crucified and men than perhaps anything else.

I understand more. The height of my tree gives me a greater, deeper, inner vision. I understand it is possible for a pilgrim of the Absolute to be at once crucified on a tree on a glorious island, and to be walking the earth in search of Christ in other men. In fact, unless these pilgrims are crucified, they will not find the Lord in others.

Looking back on Toronto, Ottawa, New York and the many Harlems of the American cities, it seems that the refrain of our lives then was the chant of a beggar. Fifty years later I still beg, but this time from my island, from my cabin, in plain sight of maples turning red, singing the glory of God. I beg by mail, because it seems that the sea of the needs of mankind is rising like a tide.

Today, sitting in my little cabin on my island, I cannot see the river, nor the beautiful maples. I see only the faces of the poor in Latin America, the West Indies, Pakistan, Africa, in our rural areas, and in our vast and complex cities. These poor crowd around me. Some are silent, some are shouting, some are crying, some are moaning.

Some are old, some are young. There are men among them, and women and children. How does one beg for all these?

Such immense needs, and so few of us to fill them. New vocations come constantly to Madonna House; yet we are still a small group to venture out and spread ourselves in small groups across the world. But then, love does such things. One person can become many if he or she is in love with God and becomes the servant and lover of others.

It is a joy and a privilege to throw one's life at God's feet and sing and sing that one can bring him such a little thing! But in our day and age, giving a life is not enough. One has to have a few cents, a dollar or two, a rupee, a peso, to buy the bare necessities of life, so as then to be able to serve one's neighbors.

Yes, loving and serving our neighbor today, even in the deep spirit of physical and spiritual poverty, demands money. So I continue to beg, knocking at a thousand doors, not in person as I used to, but by letters.

Yet, I notice that as the needs and hunger of men grow, the writing of our begging letter gets harder. How does one explain and write about these ravaged faces, milk-less breasts, hungry children, pathetic and decrepit elderly? I don't know. So I pray in my log cabin, looking at the red tips of the maples. I pray to the risen Christ and the Holy Spirit to do the begging for me.

The river is quiet, reflecting a beauty that surpasses both imagination and the ability of any writer to describe. What is she waiting for? The kiss of the frost? The time of her entering into the deep silence of her winter and her God? Who can tell?

As I look out of my window I cannot help but meditate on the conditions of our times. Today, men, like the

trees, are a variety of colors. There is among Christians
an awakening from the drabness, the grayness that most of
us have been living in for several centuries now. It could
be that we render glory to God by this awakening, by this
questioning, by this hungering that suddenly has filled our
hearts with the desire to return to a life lived without compromise according to the gospel.

Those of us who feel this way may truly be the yellow,
red or golden leaves that fill the Church with the colors
that are our song, the song we sing on our pilgrimage
toward union with the risen Christ. In the background,
like the unchangeable fir trees, stands the mysterious
Church, the Bride of Christ.

Some of us, like the river, are quiet, either with the
silence of indifference or tepidity; some are just plain
waiting, reflecting, like the river, what is happening around
us; others prefer to be frozen into immobility rather than
decide to get involved in any depth. It is a strange meditation that comes to me as I look at this beauty beyond
description, the beauty of autumn in a northern land. And
as I look I ask myself the question: Is this the time of God's
visitation? Has he taken up once more the cords of his
just anger? Is he again cleansing his temple of all those
who, in some way, are desecrating it?

Who could these people be? Are they the ones whose
faces are still filled with racial hatred? Are they the violent,
the warmongers, the traders in arms? No. These latter are
the "cold" spoken of in the book of Revelation. We *know*
God's attitude towards them.

Who are they? Not those who hunger and thirst for
justice, those who have arisen on a pilgrimage of love. Nor
those who desire with a great desire to live the gospel with
their lives. These are the "hot ones" of Revelation.

Suddenly the answer comes to me: it is the *lukewarm*

the Lord is driving from his temple, the *tepid* whom he "vomits out of his mouth." They are people who are content with the letter of the law. They are those who never try to find the spirit behind the letter. They are the ones who are afraid to do so, the ones who prefer to live and teach a watered-down Christianity. They are the ones who have created unto themselves a Christ who has no resemblance to the Christ of the gospel. Yes, they are the tepid ones!

It comes to me during my meditation today that this might indeed be the time of God's vomiting the tepid out of his mouth. He desires, at long last, that his face be shown by those who hunger for justice, who pilgrim with passionate desire not only to find him but to give him to others. These, the "hot ones," will then be able to show the face of Christ to the "cold ones."

The river is quiet, reflecting the hues of the trees. The evergreens stand as an unchanging backdrop to these trees which sing to the glory of God with their variety of colors.

*   *   *   *   *   *   *   *   *   *

Let me tell you about how I acquired my Russian shrine.

Before the Second Vatican Council began, we at Madonna House had been preparing ourselves and studying for almost a year. We thought very seriously of what we were going to do in response to the Pope's request for prayer and penance. Each person settled his or her own individual matters of penance with his or her spiritual director. Prayer in common and individually was an obvious preparation.

But our hearts, filled with a great love for the Church in that hour of her deliberations, sought to do more. It occurred to us that it would be a beautiful gesture, and one in keeping with all the prayers for the unity of Christians, to build a shrine, a symbol of unity between East and West. Around the time we were thinking about this we received, from the monastery of the Holy Trinity in Jordanville, New York, a postcard with a picture of a Russian shrine on it. I was delighted, and brought it immediately to the attention of everyone.

Father Callahan, the director of the priests, got the idea of asking Mr. Nicholas Makletzoff, a Russian architect in Toronto, and a distant relative of mine, to make a blue-print for the shrine. This he gladly did. Our men went to work. On October 3, 1962, the shrine was blessed. It is beautiful to think that it had been blessed on (what was then) the feast of the Little Flower whose missionary spirit and zeal are unparalleled.

The shrine stands on the edge of my island, on a promontory that juts out into the Madawaska River. It is surrounded by a lovely wall of greenery—birch trees, berry bushes and maples. The shrine has carved, wooden columns, Russian-style. It has a large Russian icon on its wall which can be seen from far away. From the wall hangs an antique vigil-light holder, the hook for which was made out of scrap iron by one of our members, Al Osterberger. Al also made a wrought-iron cross to go above the icon of Our Lady of Kasznia.

A vigil light burned before the *Bogoroditza* day and night for the intentions of the Council. The little shrine is all wood. One can come and kneel inside it far from the inclemency of the weather, for it is enclosed on three sides. Its roof is made out of old-fashioned wood shingles. It is crowned with the typical, onion-shaped dome that is seen on top of all Russian churches; it represents Christ and his crown. It can be seen by anyone traveling by boat, or passing on our secondary highway, a symbol, we hope, and a reminder, of the unity desired by all of Christendom.

What with this lovely Russian shrine, and the Stations of the Cross I described for you, and my other small shrines to Our Lady and St. Francis, my island is a visible sign of the unity and harmony we are all praying for.

*   *   *   *   *   *   *   *   *   *

The leaves that have fashioned the green wall of my cell during the past few months have vanished and now lie lifeless on the brown earth. They are barely distinguishable from the ground. Soon they will become one with it and the snow will sing its requiem for my walls which, like all living things, had to die.

My thoughts turn to the dead, the billions of men and women who have come from the dust and who have returned to it. I think of the martyrs and saints; I think of all the sinners. My heart sings a song of joy. For as I behold the majesty of the green pines which never change through all the seasons, I think of the constant mercy of God. I know that the nakedness of the other trees which stand so forlorn and shivering now in the freezing November wind will be clothed next spring in a new dress of green. Life is stronger than death.

My island in November is revealed to anyone who passes by, due to the crumbling of my walls, but few people pass! A strange silence reigns all around me—a silence that speaks of death and at the same time sings of resurrection. A silence that speaks of the dust to which we shall eventually return, but also sings of the glorified bodies that will be ours.

Yes, I think of the billions of dead who know definitely what we only believe, and who now see what we dimly expect. But they, together with us, stand in the circle of a gray-black river, expectantly waiting for the parousia, the second coming of Christ.

I am indeed filled with longing and expectation to feel the touch of God's mercy, to hear the tenderness and feel the compassion that will be in his voice—to be enveloped with the fire of his love. November, the month when we especially remember the dead, finds so much on my island that is dead, too. But that which is dead sings of life.

*   *   *   *   *   *   *   *   *   *

I am sad today. A note of fear creeps into my meditations and thoughts. Why am I afraid? I find that I am still praying and worrying about the effects of Vatican II on all of us, but especially on us laypeople.

Some think that Madonna House is removed from the tensions, stresses, rat races of the world around us. Nothing could be further from the truth! Madonna House apostolate is right in the thick of life as it is lived in the marketplaces of our North American continent. It shares the problems of suburbia. It sweats out the crises of the old and new cities. It is involved in the problems of seminaries, convents, religious priests and sisters, married and single folk. It is neck-deep in the problems of the world through its missions and through the many people who come here from all over the world.

At times it seems to me that we are the very pulse of the world. This was especially true during and right after the Council, when so many passed through. Their problems were begotten, strange as it may seem, by the *aggiornamento* of the Church, or perhaps I should say, by the tremendous encounter of men with the wind of the Spirit that was and still is blowing across the world.

Almost palpably one could sense the long, pent-up

emotions of all sorts of Christians—especially Catholics. Protestants came, too, hopefully but somewhat fearfully. Jews came, still deeply wounded by all that had transpired between them and Christians since the death of Christ. Seminarians came filled with revolutionary ideas, good revolutionary ideas, radical ideas which, on the whole, stemmed from the gospel, from the teachings of Christ, the true "Radix."

The world came to us through its representatives—the hopeful, the frightened, the bewildered, the impatient, the delighted, the angry. We were filled, like every other Catholic center, with discussions between conservatives and liberals, each in his or her own way eager for the fruits of the Council to be implemented.

Today, as the beauty of the fall begins visibly to fade from my island, this surge occasioned by the Council comes back to me—and a certain sadness and fear come back, also. We still seem to be walking on thin ice, the kind which will be coating my river very shortly. Perhaps it is necessary for all of us to accept this challenge of walking on thin ice, with the danger of falling through!

One question worries me above all others, and yet I welcome discussion of it at the same time. It is the question of obedience. Yet, perhaps it is not so much the question of obedience as the question of making changes in the art of governing. Yes, I think the emphasis should be on that. The key, of course, is found in the truth that "to govern is to love, to govern is to serve."

Probably many adjustments will have to be made in the Church to implement this change of attitude on a day-to-day basis. I desire, with a great desire, some clarification on this issue. For me, obedience is the essence of poverty. The words of the scriptures haunt me: "He was obedient unto death, even death on a cross."

Obedience and poverty blend into one for me. I consider mere physical poverty a kind of kindergarten school in Lady Poverty's tremendous school of love. I consider obedience her crown, her postgraduate course, if you will.

I would like to see this clarification of authority and its exercise. Then, I think, obedience will remain what it always was: the closest imitation of Christ man can achieve. It is the shortcut to death to self which alone leads to sanctity. What I sense, though, is a thoughtless approach, an impatient and dangerous approach to the question of obedience in our days.

Winter

I went outside for a bit today to enjoy the first light film of snow. Sitting in my Russian shrine, I was thinking—of all things—about the rosary, the neglected, rejected rosary. Yes, there I was, praying in a Russian shrine in Canada, thinking about the rosary.

What is the rosary? It is a string of beads arranged in a certain way. I remembered my childhood in Egypt where I saw Arabs who often fingered a rosary. The Mohammedans also have a string of beads, but with a tassel at the end instead of a crucifix.

I once asked an Arab maid why the men were fingering these beads all the time. She said, "For the glory of Allah and for help in meditation." As I grew up, and traveled across the world—India, China, Europe and Russia—I saw among both pagans and Christians a variety of "rosaries," with beads arranged in different patterns on a string. Everywhere, this simple device has helped men to meditate.

We have a little gift shop in Madonna House where we sell what people donate to us. Several years ago someone donated some beautiful rosaries—a whole pile of them —and no one bought them. Until recently! The people who bought them were mostly young people, the kind the world calls "hippies." Intrigued by this fact, I asked one of them, "Why do you buy rosaries and wear them around your neck?"

The two bearded young men, and the two girls with beautiful long hair, looked at me with a slight expression of pity and amazement. My question must have seemed a bit stupid to them! They answered: "Why, to show the world that we love J. C." By this time I knew that "J. C." in their language stands for Jesus Christ. I felt a little ashamed for having asked the question.

The same young people who are reciting the Mohammedan rosary also have the Eastern rite rosary on which one can say the Jesus prayer ("Lord Jesus, Son of the living God, have mercy on me a sinner"). This prayer is becoming more and more known to the youth on this continent. But the Catholics have discarded the rosary as obsolete, as something meant for the illiterate and for children, as something utterly meaningless and irrelevant for our days!

God called to me in my Russian shrine and I returned to my cabin. But my thoughts on the rosary returned with me. What is the rosary? The rosary is the story of the Incarnation. It began in the womb of a woman who simply said "Yes" to God. The rosary follows the main events of the life of the Man-Child to whom she gave birth, and who for us Christians is God, the second Person of the Most Holy Trinity.

Step by step, in awesome simplicity, anyone can follow the life of Christ. Each decade is dedicated to a particular aspect of the life of Christ. As the drama of his life unfolds, the tempo increases. Finally, man is killing God, and God is willingly dying for love of man. The tragedy pierces heart and mind with almost intolerable gratitude. Then, slowly, the pain is assuaged by the Resurrection and the realization that the Lord is in our midst.

The problem with the rosary probably was (is) the manner of its recitation both in churches and in the home.

It cannot be hurried. Mysteries do not lend themselves to mumbling, to carelessness, to rapid recitation. No. One decade a day might be better, or even one a week. Entering deeply into the mysteries of the beads will be entering into the whole immense mystery of the life and death of our Lord Jesus Christ.

Who, better than Mary, could act as a guide for us? She was there throughout the years of Nazareth. She was there with the holy women who followed him through his short period of preaching. She was there when he was pushed around from tribunal to tribunal. She was there under that cross, and by the grave when he was buried. She was in the upper room where the 11 frightened men huddled around her. Mary "started it all" in a manner of speaking, by her "Yes." So our "Hail Marys" simply honor her for her role in these mysteries, and we ask her to lead us also through the earthly life of her Son with similar devotion and faith.

I wondered if we really know the difference between childishness and childlikeness. Have we completely forgotten what the Lord said, "Unless you become like little children, you will not enter the kingdom of heaven"?

Perhaps I am a fool, but I continue to say the rosary, though I must confess it takes me a long time to say the 15 mysteries! I have never been able to say more than one mystery a day because "saying" is not the proper word when one talks about meditating on mysteries. One is plunged into a mystery and has to stay there, waiting, until God himself slowly reveals as much of it as he desires.

Yes, I had quite a meditation on the rosary this November, and for some reason, probably because I love you all, I wanted to share this meditation with you.

* * * * * * * * * *

My Russian shrine stands peaceful and quiet. Its roof is covered with snow. The Virgin of Kiev is reflected in the vigil light that always burns before her face. It looks especially beautiful in the dark of the winter nights. Squirrels and raccoons scamper around, leaving tracks on the snow, as does my doe who comes to drink at the river where the current is too swift to freeze. Once in a while, bear tracks are also seen on the snow!

In such an environment, December comes to greet me and leads me slowly and gently into Advent, to the Expected One—the Child in the cave—the Child who is God. It isn't difficult for me to imagine that snow and ice, trees and animals, share in my expectation. In December my island sings of the coming of the Prince of Peace.

The island is bare. And there is a stillness, a holy stillness that makes very real to me the words of the Christmas antiphons, "When the night was still, your Almighty Word leapt down from heaven." My mind turns to that holy night that is always so close, though it happened almost 2,000 years ago. I cannot help meditating on this beautiful antiphon. My mind spins a cradle of silence into which the Word that leapt from heaven comes to rest.

Silence and speech, contemplation and action—these form the very heart of the Christian life. To receive the Word we must gather ourselves up, recollect ourselves. The fire of the Holy Spirit is often expressed in many revolutionary ways which seem confusing to us. But if we are silent, if we recollect ourselves and prepare to hear the voice of the Word, then we shall cease to be confused; we shall be made ready for the revolution of love.

Yes, we must become cradles of silence, meditation and contemplation, so that the Word may find our hearts ready to receive him—our souls and minds ready to hear his message of love. And, hearing it, may we arise and go forth and live it!

So startling, so naked, so direct are some of the changes brought forth by the Vatican Council that many people are still shaken by them to the very core of their being, even after all these intervening years. These feelings are apt to discourage, confuse us. But if we make ourselves cradles of silence to receive the Word, then all these feelings will be subdued by the Lord as he subdued the storm on the Sea of Galilee. Then we shall see clearly, with the eyes of love, what we must do and how we must implement the message of Christmas in our lives.

My island is bare. The water of the river is steel grey, and so is the sky. But the white, silent, peaceful snow that covers the ground teaches me to try to make out of my soul a cradle of silence so as to receive more reverently, more fully, the mighty Word that leapt from the royal throne.

* * * * * * * * * *

Around this time a few years ago, after returning from a trip, my island looked very good to me. Though all the beautiful, shimmering, golden leaves had disappeared, and every tree was naked before the Lord, I was glad to be back. I had been away on a lecture tour of 10 days to Cleveland, Youngstown, Toledo and Canton, Ohio.

It was a wonderful trip, for it brought me an award that gave much joy and consolation to my heart. Officially the award read: "Pius X Award to Catherine de Hueck Doherty, Apostle of Restoration. St. Martin's Apostolate of Christian Social Renewal." It was given to me by this group which I love so very deeply.

Behind those official words lay a thousand memories of the founder of the St. Martin's Apostolate, my old friend Joseph Newman. He had come to Friendship House in Harlem long ago and far away as a young boy. Now he is

married and has a lovely wife and family; he is also a deacon
of the Catholic Church. He and about 150 people, all connected with the interracial movement, were present at this
lovely dinner. Also, there were many former staff workers
from Friendship House and friends from those early days.
The atmosphere was gay, warm, joyous, humble and simple.
My heart truly sang my gratitude to the Lord God for this
wonderful gathering.

To describe the hospitality of the people of Cleveland
is difficult, and I shall never forget it. I was also privileged
to get a glimpse of the inner city through the eyes of some
wonderful people: a priest who labored mightily in the
cause of love and justice, young people who had gone to
live in its jungles. I was overwhelmed by the sight of a
laity truly getting involved and concerned.

In Youngstown and Canton I spoke to priests who
were making a day of recollection. They were delightful
people to talk to and very kind to me. So if any other woman
is ever invited to speak to priests, let her not be nervous.
They are not a difficult audience! Nor were the sisters whom
I addressed in Toledo. They were wide-awake women, full
of questions.

I also addressed private audiences in large numbers
and received deep insights into the awakening of the laity
in Ohio. At the same time I got a glimpse of the problems
so familiar to me. It seemed as if good and evil were engaged
in combat. I realize deeply the evils that will always ac-
company the evangelization of the world; I also realized
more fully the remedy, and it came to me in a meditation
in a convent chapel where I was staying.

Urbanization will tend more and more towards ac-
centuating Christian humanism, making men more aware
of the social evils and the need for their correction. Because
of this, they will become involved more and more in a

spiritual rat race of activity, even as the secular world is involved in the rat race of frantic activity.

It seemed to me that this could be the most subtle temptation yet presented by Satan to humanity. Such ceaseless activity would reduce men's understanding of the mystical, contemplative approach to God. It would also reduce prayer life to almost nothing.

We must remember the rhythm of salvation history. It all began in a garden. Through the fall of man, Adam was cast out. Then, God chose Abram who was a city dweller in Ur, probably one of the largest cities in the ancient world. In that city God revealed himself to Abram and led him into the desert, out of the city. Then God led Abraham's descendants back to a city, the city of the Egyptian pharaohs. But from there he led them back into the desert and finally into another city, Jerusalem. So the rhythm of salvation history leads from the garden to the city, from the city to the desert, from the desert to the city and back to the desert again. Such is the constant rhythm.

As I meditated on this rhythm I realized why it was that some years ago I was moved to build a poustinia here at Madonna House. This hermitage was mainly for our staff who were engaged in the works of the apostolate. They needed to go from the city of men to the desert, and there listen to the Word of God in the silence of God. As we see it, civilization will become more and more urbanized. It then becomes quite evident that the hearts of men will hunger and thirst for just such a place for replenishing their souls which have been emptied by the noise and tensions of the cities. Yes, city dwellers must come to the desert from time to time, so they can return to the city with greater peace in their hearts.

*   *   *   *   *   *   *   *   *   *

The river is imprisoned today in the powerful arms of a thick icy sheet that covers it completely. The air is cold, clear and crisp. Nature seems to have entered into its time of prayer and solitude, some sort of special union with God.

But what about man? In a few weeks the Christian world will celebrate the birth of Christ. What real meaning will this feast have for Christians who are so filled with struggle and pain? Not too long ago some of them—Christians!—were proclaiming that God is dead! Will Christmas, the birthday of the God they think is dead, stir their hearts in awe and wonder? Or will it pass them by unnoticed and unimportant?

As I sit by my window and watch the contemplative silence of nature, I feel a strange, deep pain. For it seems to me—how can I explain it?—that suddenly I have lost my being, that I live in the hearts of those who believe that God is dead. I live even in the hearts of those who, though baptized, do not believe that he was even born.

This strange pain becomes unbearable because I know it is not mine but theirs. I realize that these souls, into which I have been allowed to enter by my meditation, are filled with a hunger which burns and consumes them. This hunger torments and overshadows their lives, often taking the forms of restlessness, anger and despair.

They say God is dead, but they cannot, will not, bury him! They cannot bury him because they desperately want him to be alive, want to believe in him, hunger for an encounter with him.

Those who do not believe that he was born have this hunger, too. Only they suppress and deny it even to themselves. They cannot stop talking about him as they try to convince others that he does not exist! A strange paradox. Why should anybody discuss, or wish to discuss, a nonexistent subject? People normally do not discuss something or someone who does not exist. But these people do, as though something within them relentlessly drives them.

They say they are atheists, unbelievers. They spend their time proving the nonexistence of God. But in their souls is the same hunger for him. They try to satisfy it by using his name, by repeating the word "God," and then launching into proofs of his nonexistence.

My pain grows. I am crushed, almost annihilated, by the weight of that hunger and that denial, by their search and their despair.

Then I am back again in my log cabin, in the presence of the white snow, the frozen river and the green-black fir trees. My fear vanishes. Darkness falls on the white snow. Night has come, and with it my tears have come. I weep bitter tears before the icon of the Mother of God. I am glad I can weep, because in our Eastern spirituality our holy and wise men have taught us to weep over our sins and the sins of others; they also taught us to weep tears of love. They say such tears cleanse us and those for whom we weep.

I am glad I can believe this, and I thank God for the gift of tears. Perhaps, just perhaps, my weeping in the month of Christ's birthday may resurrect him in the hearts of tepid Christians, hungry Christians, the searching and the lonely. All around me my island is still, and I sense that nature, in its own fashion, seconds my hope.

* * * * * * * * * *

People sometimes ask what will I do when I "retire." Well, if I ever do, part of that time may be spent "traveling." But it will be a particular kind of traveling, the traveling of a Russian hermit. If I travel, with the permission of my spiritual director, it will be to get to a town or village or larger city, to go and pray for the people there.

What a stupid idea . . . to believe that my prayers, the prayers of a lone woman, can do anything for a city, a town or village! But then, I believe that prayer really changes things for the better, no matter who prays. Even when such an inadequate person as myself prays.

But for a Russian, prayer by itself is never enough. As my father used to say, "Lift both arms of prayer and penance to God." So, for me, it will mean going to Montreal, for instance, going into the poorest section, taking a little room and spending a week there on bread and tea, praying for the people of that city. Then I will return to Madonna House and my island.

I feel most strongly these days that we Christians need solitude, silence and contemplation. These are terribly, urgently needed, and they should be at the top of our priority list. Doesn't it say in the scriptures, "Pray without ceasing. When you pray, go into your room and pray to your Father in secret"? This, of course, means that one must enter into oneself and make a sanctuary there, for the secret place is the human heart. The life of prayer—its intensity, its depth, its rhythm—is a measure of our spiritual health and reveals us to ourselves. Isn't it the beginning of wisdom to know oneself?

The scripture also says, "Rising up long before day-break, he went out and departed into a desert place, and there he prayed." This signifies the concentration of a recol-lected and silent spirit. At this level, where man knows how to be silent, true prayer is found. Here he is "mysteriously visited," as staretz Silouan says.

Yes, as I walk around my island, I look at it with new eyes and remember these words of scripture and meditate on them. I know, from years of my own experience, that interiorized prayer, silence and solitude can be had within oneself in the midst of the marketplace, amid its noise and clamor and frantic activity. But I also know that, for me, the time has come to leave the marketplace and to bring into the light of day that which I have tried to interiorize throughout the years.

My heart is filled with gratitude to God that at long last I am able to taste the solitude, to know the stillness, to be able to pray within it for the world, but especially for the Church, for the priests I love so much, for the young people. I am grateful that I will be able to put into practice that proverb of my people: "The house of a true hermit has no latch on the door."

Why? Because no one prays for himself, not even a hermit. He exists for others. Whatever his prayers and mortifications, he must give them away, even as he must share the humble food that is his with any visitor who comes. He does not belong to himself. He belongs to everyone, and so he must not only share his food, but his thoughts, the graces that God may give him, and above all himself. Yes, I am grateful to God for my solitude whereby I can give myself to the whole world.

In the midst of barren trees and the freezing river, all around me is the spring of the Lord. For I was meditating today on the fact of how many people are finding their spiritual legs, their spiritual home, their spiritual identity in Madonna House. The numbers that continue to come to us are simply incredible! I thank God for this wonderful privilege of hospitality that is ours. Today, in our homeless world, poverty-stricken countries are in need of housing. But so are all of us. It came to me that each one of us in Madonna House is a kind of home for the homeless.

Besides people needing physical homes, millions need spiritual homes, need to find themselves, to be accepted as they are, loved, welcomed. That is what a home is for. All of us should meditate on being homes for the spiritually

homeless. It is such a beautiful meditation, and it has such
infinite depths to it. It is a good meditation for this month
of December when there was no room for the Lord in the
inn. May all of us become homes for the homeless.

Then all our winters will be turned into springs.

*   *   *   *   *   *   *   *   *   *

Whenever I cross the bridge to my dark island, I see
dimly, then quite clearly, my vigil light twinkling through
the large window. It is the only moving sign of life on
my island.

There is a deep mystery in "coming to the island." One
feels that one is coming into a place of quiet or rest, leaving
behind the hustle and bustle of the world. Yet, one has also
the feeling that there is some very important task that will
have to be attended to when one reaches the island, a task
that cannot be done on the mainland with its constant,
ever-increasing tempo of life, its demands on all of one's
attention, as well as its tendency to confuse and diffuse
mind and soul, tiring them somehow.

As I cross the black, icebound river, I begin to understand that indeed I am going away from men to God, to
rest in his silence, to pray at his feet. My task here is to
recollect myself so that tomorrow I might return to men to
love them and serve them for Christ's sake, for God's sake.

I begin to realize, too, that I have yet another task to
perform on my island: I must set my mind at rest and quiet
my heart—detaching it from all created things in order to
turn it to God, the Creator and the Lover.

This is what islands are for. Not everyone has an
island to live on, to come from, to go to. But all of us must
make our own islands within our hearts. Islands where fear
cannot dwell. Islands where we can cross over the bridge

of our days to rest at the feet of the Beloved, to drink of his silence, to be made whole again and ready for the battle of tomorrow.

Not everyone can be a contemplative religious. Not everyone is called to that very special and high vocation. But we all need a place to rest and be silent before God so as to hear his voice speak to us in that silence. All of us, if we really understand and desire, can make our own islands within us. One can nightly "cross over the bridge" to this place apart. If we do, our days will be full of the fruitfulness of the Lord and of his peace.

Yes, life should be a daily coming from our islands to the mainland, and of returning from the mainland to our islands. I thank God every day for my island.

* * * * * * * * * *

The fir and the pine branches bow humbly under the weight of the snow—my thoughts turn to purity of heart, the purity the Lord spoke of in his beatitudes: "The pure of heart shall see God."

Human hearts are like the snow. They can be cold and heavy if one tries to examine them, touch them, weigh them. Such hearts can be likened to hearts of stone which are also cold and heavy, closed to the grace of God, drawn inward like the branches that are weighed down with the burden of the snow.

But if one looks with faith at the work of God in nature, then the snow is a gift of God, a symbol of virgin hearts, humble hearts whose earthly garments, though shabby, clothe the sons and daughters of the King.

I look at the shining trees; purity of heart and virginity of soul belong to those who know that they are the poor ones of the Lord, who realize that of themselves they are nothing, and that everything comes from him.

The Lord bends the green fir branches down, as he does us, his creatures. It is good to know that we are creatures, to know that we are nothing without the Lord. It is good to turn our minds, hearts and souls humbly and trustingly to God.

Purity of intention makes life and all the world snow-white with beauty; it brings men the grace of being able to love God and neighbor more. Let us praise the Lord as the trees and the snow praise him on my island!

*   *   *   *   *   *   *   *   *   *

The blue river, now turning steel-black, slowly surrenders to being frozen into a white immobility and silence.

It seems that mankind today is imprisoned in the ice of doubt, bewilderment, confusion, insecurity and fears. And yet, the mercy of God sends the Son of faith and love to banish all fears and confusion. Perfect love casts out all fears and all allied devils.

But the sparkling ice speaks also of the hope and trust that should fill us Christians. These attitudes could grow within us if we only let them. They would help us walk through any kind of spiritual landscape which the Lord might use to bring us to himself.

*   *   *   *   *   *   *   *   *   *

The mountains in the background almost blend with the dark skies.

Our spiritual journey will end on a mountain, for the Lord dwells on a mountaintop. But the journey through those mountains might be made among stark naked trees, along dark, forbidding paths. We must be prepared to walk.

It is thus that the Lord teaches us to become aware of his love and mercy—teaches us to rely less on ourselves and more on him.

It seems to me, as I sit by my window at eventide, that what we need is a true encounter with our Brother, Jesus Christ. We need to open ourselves completely to the work of the Holy Spirit so as to find God the Father in whom alone is our peace, our security, and our joy. It seems to me that we must enter into the silence of Mary, the little, simple, holy Jewish maid who knew so well how to repeat her *fiats*. They made every moment of her day secure in her trust of God, even though there were a thousand things that she did not understand but which she kept in her heart, in faith.

Silence will heal the wounds inflicted by the endless words that swarm around us, exhaust us, tire us beyond all tiredness. We need silence in our noisy, work-filled life, as a child needs its mother's milk. We need to be alone with God. We need to have a desert, be it only a corner of some apartment, some house, where we can go and rest with God. We need to follow him to some hill, to some garden where he himself was also wont to pray when he was tired and weary and distressed.

We need silence in order to be able to listen to our brothers, to listen with the heart. We need silence to open our souls to our brothers, making an inn for the thousands who may be living in palatial homes but have no place to lay their heads of loneliness. We need that silence to be able to speak a few words charged with our love, charged with Christ.

*　*　*　*　*　*　*　*　*　*

A fog surrounds my island today. It is one of those strange, somewhat mysteriously depressing days that come to our mountains. It makes the rivers and lakes and everything look out of proportion. I call them my days of temptations. Fog distorts, and distortions confuse and even frighten one. Therefore, my companions on a foggy day like this seem, for a while, to be Confusion, Chaos, Distortion and Fear.

But today, I seem to be especially burdened by my invisible, though quite tangible companions. Strangely enough, while the fog cuts off my natural vision, it seems to clarify my supernatural one.

I see the Church. I see myself and all of us Christians, the people of God who have been baptized in the Lord. But why do I suddenly understand that the Church is so much more than the laity, the priests, and the magisterium? Why do I understand that the Church is also a mystery? Why do I tremble with fear as I consider the call of Vatican II to bring this Church back to the marketplace where it started, to bring back the participation of the laity to whom the Fathers of the Council dedicated a whole document in their pronouncements?

The fog gets thicker on my island. It slowly begins to evaporate in my mind and heart. But I am still afraid. I'm afraid that we, the laity, are beginning to treat the Church as if it were another business venture, like General Motors or the Bell Telephone Company. We believe that we are going to restore it, reorganize it, put it on its feet by our own intelligence and by our own tremendous know-how!

But the Church is not the Bell Telephone Company, it is not General Motors. Primarily the Church is a mystery! She is the Body of Christ. If we treat her as if she were a business outfit, we will hack this Body into small pieces and crucify it piece by piece on a grotesque, misshapen cross.

If the Body is crucified in that way—the Body which we are—then we shall again crucify the Head who exists with the Body, and without whom the Body cannot exist.

The Church is the Body of Christ through which his divine life flows into us. She is also his Bride, and therein is the mystery which is not totally comprehensible to our minds. How can the Church be both Bride and Body at the same time?

The fog outside thickens. It is hard now even to distinguish the trees on the opposite shore. But the fear and confusion within me are beginning to dissipate. The natural fog is thick. The fog within is scattered by the presence of Christ who promised to be with his Church until the end of time.

* * * * * * * * * *

Christmas day in Combermere this year was crisp and cold . . . the temperature around 12 below zero! The green pines and fir trees were silent with the silence of recollection and expectation. Not a needle on their regal branches moved. Not a thimbleful of heavy snow that decorated a branch fell. The skies were clear, light blue, the special winter blue that is seen only in the North.

The grounds of Madonna House were crisscrossed with paths which made an intricate pattern of shadows and lights both under the brillant sun and the winter moon. The path to my new bridge was wide. The snow crunched gaily even under the soft mukluks I wore. (I used to have another bridge, which I told you about before. This old bridge was a thing of unsurpassed beauty, especially in the evening when the moon made lovely designs on its railings. In the middle of the bridge I had an old lantern that shed its soft light far across the river, a token of my love to the lonely

travelers and pilgrims of life; I pray for them as I cross and
recross my bridge each day.)

Before the outdoor shrine of St. Francis a tall candle
had been stuck simply in the snow-buried well. I had put
it there to pray for all those who had asked me to pray for
them on that Holy Night. I am sure that the Lord hears
me, for the candle burns through the night, aglow in the
dark.

St. Catherine's Hermitage (did I tell you that this is
the name of my *isba,* my cottage?) was decorated by both
God and man. White and sparkling was the snow that
covered its dark roof. Shining, too, were the long icicles that
hung all round about it from the roof's edges. Frosted in
intricate designs were the wide windows; yet they still
allowed one to see from inside the frolicking golden angels
I had pasted on them. The beautiful, heavy, handmade oak
door was framed in multicolored lights, and the steps were
covered with a slight film of snow. All these decorations
made a fairy-like jewel of my humble log cabin.

Do you love candles and vigil lights? I do. Candles are
symbols of Christ the Light. Ever since I was a child, candles
fascinated me. The more so that in my time there were no
colored candles, except to put on the Christmas tree. Yes,
I grew up in the era of candles on a Christmas tree, and are
they wonderful! Soft, twinkling, shining, singing, they are
a living song to the Christ Child even as they burn themselves out for him.

Normally there were no colored table candles, only
plain wax ones, usually made at home by ourselves. Never
did mother light a candle, be it for a Holy Day, or just a
party, but it was lit for the intention of someone. Had you
come to our home on a Christmas night, candlelight would
have greeted you from every corner.

This Christmas, in St. Catherine's, two vigil lights,

green and red, burned before the little crib on top of my file cabinets. I always have my crib there. One can arrange the file cabinets to look like the hills of Bethlehem by covering them with a dark greenish-brown material.

It seemed to me that the little Infant would enjoy gay, colorful Christmas tree balls, the fragile, glass kind all children love. The world was kind of dreary and dark, so, to cheer him up, I put a lot of those gay baubles around the crib, with angels that I collect year in and year out. The two vigil lights burned for the Pope and the Church, just to remind the Lord that they need his help more than ever the coming new year.

On a dresser stood my little Christmas tree. Fresh from the forest and smelling sweet, it was decorated only with tinsel and colorful bulbs. On the big table, laden with homemade goodies that members of our family lovingly baked, stood two large white candles. They were lit for each and every one of my dear readers, past and present. The mantelpiece had four slender candles around another beautiful little crib, a gift from Germany. These burned for the Church of Silence everywhere. On the windowsill a big, fat, white candle burned for the wayfarers and all the lonely and sick of the world who are seeking God.

Before Our Lady's painting a blue vigil light flickered for all those who have helped us through the years, our benefactors. In front of Catherine of Siena, a golden light burned for the souls in purgatory. Before St. Francis, another for the missions and our apostolate. Yes, had you walked in with me to my *isba* on that holy night you would have truly seen the candles praying. Just to sit down and watch them, and the humble yet gay scene they illuminated, is to know a little better the mystery of Christmas—Love becoming a Child for the love of us.

Truly it was a silent night, a hallowed night. As I

prayed the psalms of the day—how beautiful these are too—
I wondered about people everywhere and hoped that each
was on his or her own island, all connected with the bridge
of love with one another, all filled with the song of the Holy
Night and the graces of him who chose to be born on it.

＊　＊　＊　＊　＊　＊　＊　＊　＊　＊

The other night I watched a television program:
"Modern Mysticism." It dealt first with Dr. Timothy Leary,
the famous advocate of LSD, the man who maintains that
this drug culture is truly a religion! He was followed by a
man with a shaven head who represented Satan, with head-
quarters, I think, in San Francisco or some California town.
Then, in rapid succession, we were exposed to witchcraft,
Zen Buddhism, yoga, and various other Eastern phenomena.
In-between somewhere were sensitivity courses, and the
reason for each technique was explained.

It was an interesting program, yet an exceedingly sad
one! Sad, not because so many "mystical experiences" of
good and evil were presented, but because the contemplative, mystical, *Christian* experience was so conspicuously
absent! Who can deny that we have a Christian mysticism?
Christian men and women, down through the ages, have
made "contact with God" without the help of drugs. Or
perhaps we should say that they opened their hearts to the
"contacts" God made with them.

Why aren't we represented on those programs? Modern
man is hungry for God, hungry for the supernatural. He
is desperately alone, and seeks desperately for Someone
greater than himself to whom he can pledge his total
allegiance.

He searches for this Someone, and his search leads
him into every religion and every offshoot of religion. Hun-

grily he grasps at anything offered to him. He looks at stars and signs and symbols that belong to another age, that seem to be not of our present "age of reason" or "age of technology."

I must confess it was strange to behold the young people who chanted the Krishna song. There they were, nice American girls and boys, walking down the street of a busy city, chanting their lovely song to God (as they understood him), dressed up in the special costume of their sect. The men had shaved their heads, leaving a little tuft at the back, which is consciously significant of being "different."

(All these things happen while members of Christian churches, and especially priests, nuns and ministers, vie with one another to dress in any way *but* the one traditionally associated with their ministry or their dedication!)

But dress and costume, religious habits or clerical clothes, are not that important. What is important is that humanity is seeking God. Humanity is looking for the spiritual, and the answers are coming from everywhere except from the Christians. No, it is not a question of professional Church people. It is a question of *you* and *me*. What are *we* doing about it? Why aren't *we* leading these young people who are milling around the marketplace of everyone and anyone's mysticism? Why aren't *we* leading them up the mountain of the True Lover, the Lord Jesus Christ? This mission is inherent in our baptism. Each Christian is an apostle, sent by God to proclaim the good news of the kingdom.

We just finished celebrating Christmas, the Incarnation of the Lord. He came to us because he loved us—that is the good news. That is what we must tell others. His love would enrapture, excite, enthuse all those who are really seeking, all those pilgrims of the Absolute who are walking up and down this earth of ours.

And it would captivate them, excite them, if we Christians incarnated Christ's love. Then all who saw it would repeat, like the pagans of old, "See how those Christians love one another." We would draw them to the Lord Jesus, who loves them so very much.

But we are absent from these seekers. I walked up and down my island after that program, because our responsibility is so tremendous. We cannot dodge it! Among Christians there are discussions, recriminations, accusations, hostilities, fits of anger. What kind of witness is this? It appears to others as if the "people of God," the Christians are at loggerheads with one another. These modern seekers know that we are far from loving one another; they go elsewhere for their spiritual nourishment. They say to themselves: "Look how those Christians pass the buck!"

It was getting late. The stars were out and a sliver of a moon shone overhead. I returned to my cabin after walking, but sleep would not come. I kept wondering: "The Lord has given us such Bread and Wine in abundance; why do we not share it with all those who are hungry?" We do not have a mysticism that superficially appeals to people's emotions, but we have the Mystery of Love itself! We can offer to our brothers and sisters the incredible, fantastic, Mystery of Love, Jesus Christ! If only we allowed Christ to grow in us so that with St. Paul we could all say, "I live now, not I, but Christ lives in me." Then we could offer ourselves to our brothers and sisters. Our offering will be his love blending with ours, a table of truly mystical food that will satiate all those who are seeking.

*   *   *   *   *   *   *   *   *   *

A strange thing has happened in Combermere, and on my island as well. The blue jays are so few in number that my feeding stations need replenishing only once a week. The number of squirrels that usually abound on my island has been reduced. (I see one now who looks forlorn and lonely as he comes out to warm himself in the wintry sunshine.) The farmers hereabout are wondering what happened to the birds and wild animals—usually plentiful in the winter since they do not hibernate.

My island is quiet with a strange quiet. It somehow brings fears into my heart, fears and a strange, inexpressible sadness. Is the culprit strontium 90, that element which falls down in such quantities when atom bombs are exploded? Is it possible that, before the "silent spring" that Rachael Carson predicted, we already have a "silent winter"?

Like my ancestors Adam and Eve, I was made to live with the wild animals, and, in a sense, to defend them. They form part of that paradise that was lost to us until the Christ Child came. Yet, God allowed us the company of animals even after he closed the doors of paradise. Animals and birds were to be our companions, our joy and our food. What are we human beings doing to them and to ourselves?

Miss Carson's book gave an answer to what man does to himself and to his environment. If we continue to interfere with nature, the next to go will be the trees, then the grass, then the wild flowers. And even without any atomic bombs, we shall live in a desert of our own making. We shall kill ourselves slowly by the thousand and one poisons that we administer to ourselves through pesticides, chemical fertilizers, tranquilizers, euphoriants and the rest.

Once again man thinks that he is God. All men who deify men, and all civilizations that go along with that deification, shall perish. We who have produced a tremendous technological civilization, we to whom space is becoming a familiar place, are we about to perish by playing

God to nature and ourselves, worshiping ourselves? Isn't it time that we should fall on our knees and acknowledge our dependence on God? With tears in our eyes and with the beating of our breasts, let us beg God's forgiveness and start all over again in grave humility. For somewhere, in some scientific laboratory far removed from my island, a few men are playing god, as if it were a game. They are mixing chemicals. Then they package or bottle them and hand them over to Greed and Selfishness to make hoards of gold and silver by selling them.

The sight of a bird or the scampering of a squirrel used to give joy to my heart. They still do—only there are now fewer of them to break the sadness and fears with which my heart is filled.

What is this madness that touches my island and all the countryside roundabout? I know the name of that madness, but I am afraid to speak about it above a whisper. It has many names. The first is Pride, the second Greed, and the third Selfishness. It echoes the old cry, "I will not serve."

Well, if we continue to do what we are doing, we shall create for ourselves a "silent hell."

*   *   *   *   *   *   *   *   *   *

I have learned to distinguish many kinds of rain since I've come to live on my island.

There is the soft spring rain that barely ruffles the river, but seems to fall through the surface, blending almost immediately with its swift or lazy currents. It makes me think of the gentle rain of grace that constantly falls from the Lord through the hands of Mary into the souls of men. This rain of grace is always renewing and life-giving, whereas the waters of discontent—temptations and storms—are forever playing havoc with our souls.

Then there are the violent rains that fall from the skies during summer storms, pelting the waters of my river relentlessly, as if wishing to wound or hurt it. They wound the earth, too, leaving it scarred with gullies. They remind me of the temptations that men do not fight off, temptations which pounce upon them suddenly with great violence, leaving scars in their souls. Then they must wait for the gentle rain of grace to come again and make them whole.

There are steady, cold rains that fall like a sheet of water from low black clouds, fall relentlessly day after day, in a mournful dirge that sets human nerves on edge and makes one think of souls in torment, crying in the night, crying endless tears about lost youth, lost innocence, and lost lives. They make me think of heaven weeping over such souls . . . make me think of death—not of the shining, beautiful death of souls in the state of grace, but of souls dying in mortal sin. There is a hopeless quality about this rain that fosters thoughts of hell, the only place I know without hope.

When these late autumn rains fall, through what appears to me endless days and nights, I begin to understand the enormity of mortal sin, its hopelessness and torment. These are the nights when I understand a little better the pain of Christ in Gethsemani and the need for atonement. These are the nights when I cannot sleep and almost cannot pray. These are the nights when I offer to the Lord of Hosts my sleeplessness, my pain—the strange agony that fills me, the burning desire for atonement that scares me.

There are rains and there are rains, and each kind teaches me the truths of God.

* * * * * * * * * *

Today the bright sun falls on the white snow, making it shimmer and bring forth the thousand lights hidden in its whiteness. It almost blinds you if you keep looking too long at its glory. The sun also casts a long shadow of trees and bushes upon the snow, making a kaleidoscope of patterns that no artist could readily imitate. The temperature outside is still below zero these days. Truly, my island today is a place of beauty, of light, and of joy. It is trying to teach me something new again, and I have to be silent to hear its voice.

Some years ago we received a very large, plain cross in donation. It was very well made and our men, at my request, painted it black and nailed it to a lovely, big pine tree that stands right in front of my large windows. Every morning, when I pull the curtain back, the first sight that greets me is the cross, the black cross nailed to a tree.

The cross is not frightening at all when placed in its proper surroundings. When my soul is as peaceful as my island, my faith will grow as tall and as straight and as strong as that pine tree. Then faith will be strong enough to bear the secret of the cross—and all its beauty.

One year the men of our apostolate presented me with a lovely Christmas gift. It was a beautiful, old-fashioned, Old World shrine, decorated with a colorful design and topped by a small yellow cross that sets off the dark wood of which it is made. This shrine was nailed (as a surprise to me) onto another tree, facing my black cross.

A wooden Virgin is in the shrine, carved from driftwood by a retired seaman who found it on the seashore in Portland, Oregon. He never took any carving lessons, but the statue is beautiful and well-proportioned. The exquisite sheen of wood has been polished by the waves of the sea and by long summers of warm sunshine.

Every time I come into my island I can see Our Lady

standing in her new shrine, blending with the woods all around her. At her feet is the birds' feeding station that brings them down constantly from their hideouts in the trees. Often they perch on Our Lady's shrine as if to teach me that the quickest way to find Jesus is through Mary.

Simple truths, silently imparted for me to write about. That is what my island teaches me today.

* * * * * * * * * *

It was sunrise. The distant hills were already bathed in gold and red that descended, in an incredible mixture, down to the blue ice of the river, splashing it with every shade of red and gold.

I stood spellbound! I am sure that if a painter were to paint this scene which my eyes beheld, people would say he was a crazy man, a surrealist, an impressionist, an artist that no one could understand, because this sort of thing was not to be believed. It just couldn't happen! My eyes beheld this splendor, but my mind refused to absorb, apprehend or accept it.

As the sun rose, and the incredible coloring slowly faded and finally vanished, my island and the frozen river returned to normal. I realized that the Lord had given me a lesson, an insight, some sort of veiled understanding as to what we Christians have to face in this diaspora situation of ours.

It is becoming more evident every day that we are a small handful of people in a tremendous and alien sea of atheism, materialism, secularism, and plain ignorance, indifference, paganism. We are like the Jews of old—small, ghetto-like groups, lost in the midst of many Romans and Greeks.

We have to face ourselves first of all. If we are to

restore this world to Christ we must first find out how deep, how powerful the impact of our pluralistic society is on us Christians. We seem to suffer from a spiritual malady that prevents us from burning with zeal for our Father's house, from allowing the charity of Christ to urge us on, from entering that society, from bringing love into it.

It came to me at that moment of reflection that our prayer for the 1970's and beyond should be, "Lord, I believe, help my unbelief." We have received the gift of faith in our baptism; divine life courses in us, grace is given to us, and we feed on the Body of the Lord. Nevertheless, our faith is weak.

In some strange, incomprehensible manner, our technological age and all the tremendous advances of science have affected us. We examine everything with our intellect and we believe only what we can understand, examine, weigh and analyze. This we cannot do with God. We must enter into the darkness of faith to find him, to meet him. Unless we have this personal encounter with God, our faith will remain weak and the forces from without will weaken it still more.

Prior to that sunrise, I had not believed that such beauty existed. So it is with faith. We only believe half-heartedly. God is not personal to us. He is someone remote whom we must worship, adore and obey. We do not see him in our neighbor, as we must, if we would truly belong to him.

We believe that he is in the Holy Eucharist, and yet our belief is cold and distant, instead of warm and personal. We approach Communion reverently, but never passionately, eager to become one with our Creator, one with the Tremendous Lover, one with him who is, who died for us, who walked this earth for us, who was born for us, who loved us first.

And because of this the number of Christians in the diaspora dwindles, for we need today a flaming faith, a faith that in truth moves mountains, that translates the presence of Christ into every action.

That kind of faith will send us to the ends of the earth to bring to others the glad tidings of his love. That kind of faith will remove our hesitancy as we encounter our next-door neighbor. That kind of faith will make ordinary, drab human lives things of splendor, a shouting of the Good News and the living of the gospel of love again.

*   *   *   *   *   *   *   *   *   *

Guests who come to Madonna House marvel at the beauty of what they think is for us a "Shangri-la," a retreat from the secular world—a dropout from reality. But they do not think this for very long, because *they find the essence of reality here.* They find people who try to make a community of love among themselves before they attempt to enter the very heart of the secular world and witness to the love of Christ. One wonders why so many priests, nuns and laypeople come to such an "unreal" place in an unending stream!

Why do they come? They come to bring the secular world and its infinite and varied problems to us. They come to find answers, to find rest, to find silence, to find time to think.

What do they find when they come here? They find a complex of houses and cottages and people inhabiting them. They find that all the doors of Madonna House are open to them. They find that no one is asking them personal questions but rather that they are received with joy and love. Madonna House believes that strangers are simply "friends we haven't met yet" and "other Christs."

What do they find when they come here? They find
that Madonna House is a training center for a lay apostolate.
Young people come here, attracted by this vocation. They
look it over, then accept or reject it. If they accept it, then
some sort of training begins.

There is some academic training, and much practical
training, but the real training of Madonna House is this:
it endeavors to form that community of love among its
members that will justify their going out to form communities of love with others. For how could we love the
people to whom we go if we did not love each other first?

The second part of our real training is what I call
our "open door" aspect. Every year, thousands of people
come to Madonna House. Being hospitable and charitable
to all these people is part of our training. To open oneself
totally to another within one's spiritual family is not easy;
to open oneself to everyone, to be utterly available to give
each guest not only the hospitality of our homes but the
hospitality of our hearts—this is to enter the school of the
love of Christ. It is to endeavor to preach the gospel with
one's own life.

The world is hungry for God. Some know it and some
don't. But the majority are in search of answers to that
hunger, and many come to Madonna House seeking the
answers. There are no verbal answers these days, only
existential answers, answers lived out by an individual or
group of individuals who really believe that it can be done
and who are willing to try. For they know that in trying
they will share the wounds of Christ; to love is to be crucified. But they also know that modern man in search of
God is a replica of St. Thomas the Apostle who had to
touch Christ in order to believe.

It is cozy and warm tonight in my one-room log cabin.
The vigil lights are flickering. A shaded lamp is burning.

The oil stove is singing its eternal song of heat and warmth. Peace and quiet with their loving mantle envelop me like the mercy of God.

My meditations center often on the bridge that joins my island and myself to our mainland. In the world there is a lack of bridges. I begin to realize more and more that here lies the work of the Christian.

We are bridge builders, we who dedicate ourselves to the apostolate of the marketplace. Strangely enough, the materials out of which we must build those bridges between man and man, and the tools we must use, are one and the same: love.

Love alone is the material of the bridge and its tools. For love alone will give the know-how, will enable us to break through the barriers that man erects against man. It can conquer the fears that man has towards man. Yes, love alone will do that. And the training of Christians, therefore, is simple. They must open their hearts wide and never close the doors, always allowing love to stream from their hearts . . . always, no matter where they are or what they are doing.

*   *   *   *   *   *   *   *   *   *

One year I left my Canadian island for an island lost in the warm waters of the Caribbean sea. It was Carriacou, to which I and one of our priests, Father Briere, went for three weeks to make a visitation of our mission there. So, for once, I wrote from another island, an island drenched with sun, where the tradewinds constantly blew a cooling, singing breeze that made even the warm tropical night cool and pleasant to sleep in.

This island has two seasons, the dry and the rainy, and yet both seasons are gentle to man. The temperature

never rises above the 80's, and the tradewinds temper ca-
ressingly even that pleasant temperature. It is an island
where fruit is abundant in all seasons and where the variety
is extraordinary; where the sea furnishes all the fish that man
could eat or want.

I wrote that month from the house of Our Lady of
the Islands, which is the name of our mission there. Trudi
Cortens is the director, and she has a faithful team of six
women. All of them have done and are doing a tremendous
apostolate of love on that lovable island. Strange as this
may seem, in Carriacou I could touch love; I could feel it.
I could see it in the eyes of the people. A wonderful elderly
lady said to me about our team: "They are to me like my
mother's daughters," which was her gracious way of saying
that they were like sisters to her. Wherever I went on this
beautiful island, I heard of the love that the people had for
our team, and from our team I heard how much they love
the people.

As I sat in the cooling breezes of the tradewinds, in an
old-fashioned house with high ceilings and big windows, I
knew with the knowledge of my intelligence and my senses
that any Christian apostolate must begin, continue and, in
a manner of speaking, end with an encounter, a personal
encounter with the other. Yes, we teach catechism and we
nurse on the island, and we have discussion clubs with
youth. But we have a chitchat apostolate that is one of
our joys, a peaceful, quiet visiting with the people of the
island who have become our people, our friends.

At the time of my visit a new development was about
to take place. We opened a handicraft center there and we
emphasized the cooperative movement: credit unions, pro-
ducers' co-ops and other cooperative enterprises. But all
our apostolic work along the lines of *Mater et Magistra* and
Pacem in Terris began and will continue on the basis of

person-to-person relationships, on a basis, that is, of love and friendship; otherwise, all will be unsuccessful.

Carriacou is in dire need of help—self-help, too. Its youth emigrate to USA, Canada and England, often leaving young children behind to be brought up by grandparents. There are not enough jobs on the island, and yet, there could be so many. This island needs ideas, new ideas, as the whole of the West Indies needs them; they are ready to receive them. For it is a land of much promise. It could export not only its beauty, but also its spices, fishes, and a thousand other fruits and plants.

Yes, Carriacou, as well as the other islands of the West Indies, needs fraternal, loving help from other countries that humbly, lovingly must give that help. The brotherhood of man under the fatherhood of God truly can become a reality. But in this setting, God seems to be waiting with some sort of extra impatience (loving impatience, if I may put it so) for men to come and help their brothers here where so few could do so much.

It was beautiful and wonderful to visit that other island which I had to leave all too soon. But I have taken it with me for the rest of my life wherever I go, for its gentle people have truly won my heart forever. And I am glad and happy that a team from Madonna House is there to serve them for years to come.

* * * * * * * * * *

All is still with the stillness of death. Yet, outwardly, nature, even in death, is beautiful. I find myself strangely tense and alerted spiritually as I walk back and forth across my bridge from the island to the mainland. I love these winters. I was born in a cold climate. But I do not like temperatures that go so far below zero that they freeze life out of nature.

Such cold makes me think of a soul in sin. People think of hell as a hot place full of fires. I think of it often as a cold place. Every Russian child knows that at a certain temperature one must never touch metal things with bare hands. The skin will be frozen off. There is some point at which intense cold burns like fire. That is how I think of hell. That's how I also think of sin. It does to the soul of man what cold does to nature, to the trees on my island, to the ice on my river and the slender, naked branches of the many bushes that surround the edge of my island where earth meets water.

Outwardly, the beauty of the place is unmarred, perhaps even enhanced by the play of the shadow and light on the snow. But, in reality, all things are still. There is no sap in the trees. Were this cold to continue indefinitely, all things would die.

So with the soul in sin. Man does not change outwardly. The beauty of his movements, the coordination of his body, the music of his voice continue as before. But inside he is dead, dead to God, hence, dead to love. Dead to life. He is like my trees and nature for the time being. It is a frightening sight to behold.

I pray for all the souls in mortal sin today, for they too are fearsome to behold. Lord, have mercy on us all!

*   *   *   *   *   *   *   *   *   *

One shadow, black and deep, falls on the white snow. It is the clear outline of a cross, which—because of the approach of Lent—makes me think of the Way of the Cross. I don't know if it's still an acceptable devotion in our *aggiornamento* times(!), but for me it always will be.

I am absorbed, engulfed and overcome by the cruciform shadow. Clearly, I see Pilate washing his hands in a golden bowl held by some young slave. The water appears to be clear until Pilate dips his long, tapering fingers into it. Then it appears to be utterly bloodred. Yet, I know that it couldn't be. Or could it?

Suddenly, Pilate disappears from my view because my bodily eyes can only see a well-etched cruciform shadow on the white snow of my island. Instead of Pilate I see Christ standing there, silent. Yet, it isn't the Christ I know from all the many images that I have seen, from all the various Ways of the Cross that I have made across the world. No, he is nothing like what I have ever seen.

He is not exactly standing still. He is in motion, suddenly dissolving and then coming together again, as if his body were composed of millions, billions of pieces—all moving, all different, yet all alike.

It suddenly dawns on me that I am seeing his Church, his Mystical Body, the people of God, and that this, his Body, is not only in motion but in a terrible agony. Yes, it is a motion of agony. My thoughts become jumbled, for lo and behold, again in some strange way, there are many Pilates who belong to that Body, and from *within it* are condemning Christ to death! Yes, they are condemning him to be crucified. They are washing their hands of him, once and for all, not realizing that the clear waters in which they appear to wash their hands are becoming red with the blood of God.

Now the agony is mine. I am involved in it totally, and I realize that it is so because I am part of that Christ, of his Mystical Body, of the people of God, part of his Church. I am the Church, too, and its agony, its pain is mine as well.

Now I know, with a deep knowledge that didn't come to me from books, that I must be crucified with him. That no matter what the Pilates of today do to Christ, by his grace

I will share his pain, his crucifixion. I will drink the bitter
cup to the last drop, the cup of agony of his Church. An
old spiritual comes to mind, and I can hear its tune singing
in my soul: "I Shall Stand Like a Tree, Unmoved by the
Waters."

Today is a cold day, yet a brilliant, sunny one. One
long-shadowed tree makes a deep, black pattern of a cross
on the snow.

*   *   *   *   *   *   *   *   *   *

Last January 5 the flu descended on Madonna House
in full force with all its vehemence. Forty of us went down
like trees felled by a hurricane. The remainder, 20 or so,
did miracles trying to run the complex of Madonna House
and nurse us, too.

That month, I had to live on the mainland and be
cajoled, nursed, and given tender loving care with the
others. It was only around the middle of February that I
returned to my island.

Strange, how sickness brought us all closer together,
how charity bloomed among us, how those who were a
little less sick helped those who were more sick, and how
everyone tried to help everyone else. As we recovered, we
thanked God for his goodness in sending us a little bout
of the flu. It showed us our weakness, and in our weakness
it showed us the strength that St. Paul always talks about
when he lists his frailties.

Physical sickness can depress us or elevate our spirits,
depending on our attitude toward it. Whatever is in our
hearts and our minds will solve the present and future of
our world. We hold the life and death of the world in our
hands.

Why is it that violence is reigning? Why is crime

rampant? Why are people frightened and whole cities decaying? Like the beat of a drum the question "Why? Why? Why?" beats at my heart and, I am sure, at the mind and heart of many of us. Then a strange answer comes: "Without me you can do nothing."

Foolish, isn't it? We have gone to the moon, but man still tries to build a tower of Babel on the earth. While we communicate electronically, we are almost deaf and dumb and mute with one another. While we go to the moon, we destroy our waters and our air on earth. And all this because we cease to believe in him who said, "Without me you can do nothing."

Yes, I live on an island, but I am not an island. The pain of my brethren, the pain of the world, is in my heart. And, for some reason I cannot explain, I only get one answer to this pain. It comes powerfully and ceaselessly: "Without me you can do nothing."

This is a strange season on my island, an in-between season. The snow is melting, and brown patches of earth, covered with old pine needles, appear, contrasting their darkness with the whiteness of the snow all around. The river has finally won its battle against the ice, and its victory song can once again be heard in the stillness of eventide.

Sometimes, when I sit by my window, I wonder if all of us are not in some in-between season. The spring of *aggiornamento* is still upon us, even after more than a decade. And the northern winds of "old ways" occasionally blow their icy forces on us, making us unsure and fearful of the gentle breezes of spring. These icy winds send us back into our old ghettos from which it is so hard, so unsafe, so threatening to emerge. I see Christians the world over battling with themselves, like spring battles with the vestiges of winter.

At these moments I kneel down, or even prostrate

myself flat on the floor, and pray. I know that against this north wind prayer is the only remedy. I pray passionately that none of us Christians, none of us Catholics, ever gives up hope. I pray that we may be firm in our faith, armed with true love, and head bravely into the face of those north winds of fear, conservatism, threats and timidity. I pray that we may go forth unafraid, in the name of the Risen Christ, to bring to all men that for which they hunger more than anything else: the love of God. I pray that we might continue, in quiet and peace, to fight for the truth, to fight for justice on behalf of all our brethren in the world.

I pray that we might understand how to conduct this fight, not in hostility to authority, not in endless dialogues that only lead to more dialogues, but in truth, in prayer, in fasting, in love—especially for those who try to hold back the uncontainable tide of love. I pray that while we fight for this truth and love we may love our enemies. I pray that we conduct this fight in the immense childlike simplicity and meekness that alone can win the hearts of men. I pray that we conduct this fight in faith, knowing that we, of ourselves, can do nothing, are nothing, because we are first of all creatures of God and depend wholly on him. I pray that we conduct this fight for God's sake, for humanity's sake, for our sake, and that we have only one goal: to hasten the Parousia and the union of men with God.

April is a strange season on my island, an in-between season. But I can feel the spring coming, and I know with an unshakable faith that in the Resurrected Christ lies also the springtime of the Church.